W9-BHK-222

THE LONG RETURN

By

BOB PORTER

#2603-4288 Grange St.
Burnaby, B.C. Canada V5H 1P2
Phone 604-433-3237 Fax 604-433-2722
e-mail   boport@intergate.bc.ca

2nd Edition August 1997   ISBN 0-9681953-O-X

i

For

Dicky (Mamma) Rakers

DEDICATION

I owe my life to these valiant people who risked their life and those of their families to hide me (and others) in Nazi-occupied Holland, 1939-1945

DICKY (MAMMA) RAKERS
and
HERMANUS (PAPA) RAKERS
(He was killed in an automobile accident in August 1945)

Frits van de Haar
Mr. and Mrs. Bos
Eep Bos,
Klaas and Ans van Middelkoop
Mrs. Baai
Vonny de Haan-Broere
Mr. and Mrs. Heitinga
Shelah and Eileen Heitinga
Doctor van Veelen
Mr. and Mrs. Cornelissen
Nellie Cornelissen,
Dirk Maljers (Langbroek)

I SALUTE ALL THE BRAVE MEN AND WOMEN WHO WERE ACTIVE IN THE DUTCH UNDERGROUND!

ACKNOWLEDGMENT

MY MANY THANKS TO THE FOLLOWING FOR THEIR HELP AND ENCOURAGEMENT IN PREPARING THIS BOOK

My wife FRAN-CLEMENCE, **for many hours of typing and editing;**

My daughter SHELLEY PORTER, TONY GREAVES, BOB FOWLER, JIM WILCOX, CAROL PATRICK, PETER EGGLETON, and BERKLEY THOMAS, **for editing;**

MEL PATRICK, **for his patience in teaching me how to computerise my material;**

MICHELLE ZION, **for her painting of the Lancaster on the cover;**

DEPARTMENT OF NATIONAL DEFENSE, for the pictures
Fig. 2e, 2f, 2g, 2h;

R. N. WOYCHUK (now deceased),
for the sketches on POW life;

BILL GUNSTON, for his kind permission to re-print his
" Introduction to so many" at the end of my story;

WYBE BUISING, **who did the researching in Holland for me;**

Table of Contents

Chapter One

September to Overseas 1943

I remember very well, when Britain declared war on Germany. It was Labour Day week-end 1939, and I was just 16 years old. The German army had gone into Poland but we had all been expecting it for a long time, as Hitler had been making a lot of speeches and was being very rough on the Jewish people. I can remember the day very clearly.

My two brothers, my sister Betty, my cousin Roy, Murial Davis (Jean Skelhorne) and I were sitting at the bottom of our basement stairs. We had just moved back to Burnaby from Surrey, where my father had twenty acres, and were talking about the war. England had just declared war with Germany. What might it mean to us? We knew Canada would be in it very soon, as we belonged to the British Commonwealth. I said, "I'm going to join up as soon as I'm old enough." Murial could not believe that I wanted to do this, and that is exactly what I did.

In April 1941, when I was seventeen, I joined the Dominion Provincial Youth Training Program. This was for the Air Force. I registered at the old Fairbanks Morse Building in Vancouver, at the end of the old

Cambie Street Bridge, to learn to be an aircraft mechanic. My mother was very displeased that I had quit school three quarters of the way through grade eleven and was a little nervous about telling my father that I had done this. My father had always been very strict, insisting that we get at least grade twelve and qualify for the University Entrance program. So when he found out he was very angry at me.

I actually joined up in September 1941, just after my eighteenth birthday. I was very proud of being in the Royal Canadian Air Force and being in uniform. I was first sent to the Toronto Manning Depot where the Royal Canadian Air Force (RCAF) had taken over the Canadian National Exhibition buildings.

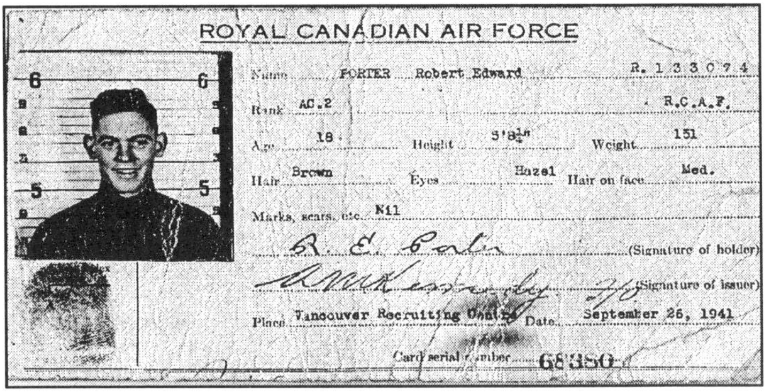

ROYAL CANADIAN AIR FORCE

Name PORTER Robert Edward R. 133074

Rank AC.2 R.C.A.F.

Age 18 Height 5'8¼" Weight 151

Hair Brown Eyes Hazel Hair on face Med.

Marks, scars, etc. Nil

(Signature of holder)

(Signature of issuer)

Place Vancouver Recruiting Centre Date September 26, 1941

Card serial number 68380

Fig.1a My ID issued 1941

These were all cleaned out and we were quartered in what was called the "Cattle Stalls." First, we were issued our uniform which came in just three sizes: large, medium or small. Then came the hair cut. I had long curly hair but it did not last long. I think I got, my crew cut about the second day I was there. I then found out about the "Short Arm Inspection," often done with female staff and whatever modesty I had was soon lost.

Myself   Fred

Fig.1b My brother Fred and I in Toronto

Finally, we all had to get our shots. Some of which really made your arm swell up. A lot of the guys passed out when they were having them. In many cases, the bigger they were the more likely they passed out. September 1941 was a really cold time in Toronto. We almost froze as we did our basic training on the parade square, with the wind blowing off Lake Ontario. During the month we were at the Toronto Manning Depot doing our basic training. I learned not to volunteer for anything. For example, the base headquarters called out on the loudspeakers for anyone that liked to drive a car. I was one of the first to step up and found myself in the motor pool, washing vehicles all day!

Myself

Fig.1c Graduation at St.Thomas Aero-Engine Mechanic

We finally left Toronto in November to move up the training ladder, first, to southern Ontario to the St-Thomas Aero-Engine Mechanics School; We finally left Toronto in November to move up the training ladder, first, to southern Ontario to the St-Thomas Aero-Engine Mechanics School; After graduating in March 1942 we were posted, to McLeod Alberta #7S Flying Training School. I was not too happy there, as I wanted to go overseas, not spending my war years fixing training aircraft on the prairies. "I was at McLeod" for about eight months, when one day, walking up to the canteen I ran into a buddy of mine. I asked him, "Where are you going?" He replied, "Up to headquarters to re-muster as air-crew."

I though that sounded great! I asked, "Do you think they will accept me, he responded," Lots of others have done it. But one needed grade twelve to get into aircrew and I had quit school in the Spring of grade eleven.

Fig.1d Anson Aircraft

However, I had finished my grade eleven maths and was working on my grade twelve maths by correspondence. Since mathematics was one of the main requirements for aircrew. I decided to go with him. The next week, they called us for an interview, to write all the tests and have our medical for aircrew. As a result, the buddy that I went up with didn't pass but I did! Probably because I was well qualified in mathematics. My report noted I was, "good average material. Should do well as a Pilot." I was always very lucky and I guess I answered the questions right. Unfortunately it gave my mother a little more to worry about.

A couple of weeks later I was off to Edmonton with those who had passed the flying training. Here I passed a winter I will never forget.

Fig.e Sitting on Anson in
in December

With a temperature of forty below even with our great coats on, we felt as if we were naked. For the next five months, we attended the Initial Training School which provided general training for all aircrew. At the end of this, we were selected to be either a pilot (first choice), navigator, bomb aimers, wireless air gunner or air gunner. I lost out on being a pilot, as I had some slight colour blindness, but I was very happy with becoming a Bombardier. A Bomb Aimer did a bit of everything. Besides being in control of the bombing, when over the target, he was also the Gunner in the front turret. In addition, he helped the Navigator with the radar and used the sextant to "shoot" stars and calculate the aircraft's position. In a case of emergency he could also take over the controls and fly the plane home.

From Edmonton, we went to No. 2 Bombing and Gunnery School in Mossbank, Saskatchewan, for bombing and gunnery training. Unfortunately, we felt that Mossbank was not only the end of the railway but the end of the world! It was the most desolate place I had ever seen. It seemed that all the girls over 16 years old had been sent to live with their grandmother in some place more isolated than Mossbank. Not many mothers were keen on their daughters going out with us aircrew because we were very carefree and were going overseas in the next few months.

I was never a church-going person but I always went to church on the first Sunday I arrived in a new town. You could almost hear the mothers say: "Look at that nice boy over there." It worked every time. The big excitement was going to Moose Jaw for the week-end. It was a lively town and always had something going on.

Finally, at the end of June, 1943, we were posted to No. 7 Air Observers School (AOS) at Portage La Prairie, Manitoba. After five weeks of navigation training, our basic flying training on the "Link Trainer" and aircrew training, we graduated and received our wings.

Fig.1f Graduation from Portage la Prairie A.O.S.

We were all posted from there, some to become Instructors and they seemed very happy, although I would have hated it. Others were posted to Coastal Command, which seemed a very safe but boring job, again not for me. I got what I wanted I was posted overseas. A few were made officers and the rest, like myself, became sergeants. We were given three weeks leave, a railway ticket to Vancouver, and a one way ticket to Halifax. We were sure proud of ourselves, with our sergeant's stripes and wings. I made a last trip to Vancouver to visit my mother in the hospital. I couldn't understand why she was crying as I said goodbye. At that time we were young, flying and going overseas. We were on top of the world and it was a very exciting time! But I can see now, mothers do not look at it the same way. I always told her: "Only the good die young and I'm not the best boy in town." On the way to Halifax, I stopped off at Toronto to visit my girl friend, Bunny, who I had met in 1941 when I was there. I was supposed to stay just a day and a half, but it ended up to be four or five days. As a result, I was a few days late getting to Halifax but the ship hadn't left yet, so I didn't get into deep trouble. Although the Air Force was a little displeased, there wasn't much they could do because they were very short of aircrew at this time. We were very naive at that young age. We thought they were making the squadrons bigger, but as they were actually losing a lot of aircraft they really never had enough air crew.

We left for England on August 27th on the Queen Mary with 22,000 of us on board. Everybody was sleeping all over the place and the dining room never closed. However we only had two meals a day, that was it. There was always a line-up waiting to eat. The food wasn't very good, but they were feeding a lot of men and I guess they couldn't do much better. I knew there would not be any liquor on the way over and we were not supposed to take anything to drink on the ship. A lot of the fellows did not drink and I knew who they were so I filled their water bottles full of Rye Whiskey. I never forgot where the bottles were.

The ocean was as smooth as glass, all the way over. We had some escort ships the first day out but, after that, we were on our own crossing to Greenoch, Scotland in five days. The other ships that went in the convoy took ten days, some of them running into submarines and many were torpedoed. The German Navy's submarine force was very strong at that time but we never saw any. The Queen Mary sailed too fast, so they never had a problem. She sailed continually back and forth through the war either from Halifax with Canadian servicemen or from New York with Americans. A few years after the war it was sold and parked in California where they made her into a tourist attraction with a fancy restaurant. Many servicemen from all over the world have fond memories of her.

Chapter Two

Bournemouth to June Sixteenth

We landed in Scotland, then went by train to Bournemouth on the south coast of England. That is where all the air crew from the Commonwealth were first stationed, all raring to go. There were air crews from all over the former British Empire, plus a lot of Americans that had come to Canada and joined the RCAF. We did a little training to keep busy and were given gas masks and clothes that we needed in England. We had more shots, in the arm or in the behind. It always seemed that when there was nothing to do, we got more shots.

The town of Bournemouth was a deluxe summer resort, which became fully occupied with air force personal during the war. The town was made up of hundreds of hotels of every size and a lot of very large homes. The RCAF had taken most of them over to billet the airmen. Every once in a while the Germans would send a few bombers over and bomb the place, which got everybody very serious about the blackout. The beaches were covered with rolls and rolls of barbed wire as well as hundreds of large concrete blocks, all laid out along the ocean edge, in case of an invasion. The blackout was very strictly enforced and not a light could be shown. All the drapes were fully pulled, with no lights allowed to show through. No car lights or bicycle lights were permitted which was very important. The Home Guard and the A.R.P. (Air Raid Precautions) went around and made sure this law was strictly enforced.

We were transferred from Bournemouth to a small holding station, Evesham, which was in south central England. We were there only a few weeks until there was room for us in Aircrew Flying Unit (A.F.U.).

Then off to Staverton, No. 6 A.F.U. which was a small air station. We were in No. 77 Air Bombing and Navigation Course. I was still with all the Bomb Aimers from the course in Canada. We had not been together for about a year by then. We had not been formed into crews, as yet. We did a mixture of bombing and navigating practice both by day and night for a month.

We were next sent to Long Marston near Stratford upon Avon, to be formed into crews. We had no choice as to which crew we were assigned but most of them worked out well. Ours was great! Our pilot was Bill Smith, known as "Smithy." We nicknamed the navigator, Bill Gardiner, "Gardy" our Wireless Air Gunner (W.A.G.) Mike Baran, was a Warrant Officer #11 (WO2). Our tail gunner was Glen Taylor and the mid-upper gunner was Sid Wilson. Bill Smith had been in England for a few years. Although he was a

Canadian who had joined the RAF and had just transferred to the RCAF. He was proud of being more English than Canadian. He had been flying Whitneys, pulling gliders around Africa, so he had a lot of experience to his credit. He was a Warrant Officer 1st class (WO1), and received his commission as a Pilot Officer soon after we met. We were very fortunate to get a pilot with that much experience. All the rest of us were sergeants except Mike Baran who was WO2.

Once we had formed a crew, we did everything together. We slept in the same bunk house which was usually a Nissen hut. We would eat together, fly together and generally go out drinking together, except Glen, who didn't drink but always made sure we got home. Sometimes in a blackout, finding one's way home could be a problem. We would even go on leave as a crew. That bonding was very important to allow us to know what each other was thinking. W e knew we were going to be in some tough spots together.

We did our crew training on Wellingtons, know as "the Wimpy". We flew all over England, and attended many lectures about the many problems we would run into. We practised in the air before making the big trip across the English Channel to make it as safe as possible. A lot of our instructors were fellows who had completed one or two tours of operations. An "Op" was a bombing trip to Germany or over occupied Europe, and a tour was twenty five to thirty trips or Ops. So few crews survived a tour without being shot down that 25 to 30 trips was quite an achievement, causing the rest of us to look up to those who had completed a tour.

In December we moved from Long Marston to Honeybourne, an operational Training Unit, to finish our training. It was here that I met my wife-to-be, Ginger. The first day I went into the mess hall, there was this cute little Welsh girl who I soon got to know. I like pepper and I was complaining that there was not that there was no pepper. One day Ginger brought a 5 pound tin and plunked it down in front of me and said "here is your goddamn pepper." We had a lot of fun together. On one of our leaves, I went home with her to Wales and they all gave me a great time. W e were married in March the next year. Things moved very fast in those days. We were enjoying ourselves quite a bit at this time. Many of us who started training in Edmonton (a year earlier) were still together. I can remember one night, Bill Ritchie, a fellow Bomb Aimer (who I'd been friendly with since we first started training in Canada), was with me in the canteen, drinking. We got feeling very good and decided to go to a dance in a small town a few miles from the camp. We were not sure of the way but we had a good idea where it was so, off we went on our bicycles! However we didn't do very well because we'd had a little too much too drink, more than we thought, and we never got to the dance. We were resting on the side of the road; perhaps we had a little sleep. Well, Bill got sick and heaved up a little, losing his false teeth on the ground. We were looking all over for them when I suddenly spotted them! Oh! too late! I had already started to take a step. You know how, sometimes when you see something while walking, your mind has already told you to take the step. Well, that's what I did, right on Bill's teeth. Of course I broke them. I think he thought I did it on purpose, but I didn't. That sort of finished the evening; the prospect of a dance was over. So, we went home. On Christmas day 1943, I was sitting in the mess feeling no pain. (I had a few too many drinks) I had gone into the kitchen (as Ginger worked there) and I got a turkey carcass to chew on. The cooks always cut most of the meat off the turkey in the kitchen and never served the bones in the mess.

Fig.2a Picture of the crew, less Bill Gardiner. Taken on Squadron

The Meteorology Officer (the fellow who tells us all about what weather to expect) and I were discussing his job. I said: "The only thing you can tell us accurately was why it had rained the day before." He and his pals promptly tossed me out of the window. I was glad it was on the first floor, and that I had had a few drinks, so it didn't hurt me.

Two nice things about being stationed in Longs Marston were firstly, courting Ginger, and secondly, I knew all the mess staff very well. So, if I ever overslept in the morning I could always get breakfast in the kitchen, even after the dining room was closed. There were always a few little extras one could get. The instructors and senior NCO's were mostly RAF types and they did not think it was right for senior NCO's to be fraternising with the female staff in the mess. But that never stopped me!

One night we went to town to do a little pub crawling. We had arranged for a taxi to take us home because, if you didn't arrange it ahead of time, you couldn't get one. After a few drinks, we got confused between the Black Swan pub and the White Swan pub where we were to meet the taxi. In the end, we were waiting at the wrong Swan and never did see our taxi. As we started walking back to base, we ran into the station ambulance just a little way out of town. The driver was waiting for the medical officer called the "MO" who was a bit of a boozer. We told the driver that the MO had gone home a long time ago, so he said to hell with it and went back to base, and taking us back with him in the ambulance. The MO was very mad but never found out who told his driver that story. It was eight miles and the MO had to walk.

Our graduation flight was a trip to France, to give us a little experience flying over enemy territory. Our first mission was to deliver leaflets telling the people

what was going on in the war, as the Germans' explanation was far from the truth. It was also an effort to
divert the German fighters away from the main
bomber stream that night. We therefore headed
across to Southern France while the main bombers
headed north. The Germans would direct their interceptors toward us, while we would drop our leaflets
and head back to England before they got to us. The
mission was similar to a bombing run but only a short
distance inside enemy territory.

Our first trip was sort of scary. There was full radio
silence and no lights. You really felt all alone. When
you saw the first big searchlights in the distance and
the first anti-aircraft flak exploding in the air, you
knew you were not over friendly territory. We felt
sure that every shot was aimed at us. When one crew
got lost and broke radio silence, the Germans homed
their guns on them and shot them down. It was awful
to get "the chop" in training, before you even
reached a squadron. However, with our youthful confidence we all knew it was going to happen to someone else, not to us. Our trip to deliver the leaflets did
not work out so well. The bomb bay doors were supposed to open, then the container should have
opened, to let the leaflets drop out. Instead, the whole
container dropped out. So, I have often thought of
that night, imagining some poor Frenchman looking
up in the sky to see the leaflets coming down, con-
tainers and all.

We were now finished with the Operational
Training Unit and were ready to go to a conversion
unit for experience on four-engine bombers. We

next went north to Yorkshire where we started converting to Halifax bombers. The conversion was almost finished when along came the Canadian Mark 10 Lancaster bomber, the newest four-engine bomber on which, we now retrained. They were brand new and smelled like a new car.

We took many chances, probably because most of us were under twenty, Bill Gardiner, Glen Taylor and I were just twenty-years old, while Bill Smith, who was twenty-eight was considered real old. It was great to be young and dare-devils! For examples Bill Baran, our wireless air gunner, liked to take pictures. One day we were on a practice flight near the Cliffs of Dover and he wanted to get some pictures of the birds nesting in the high, steep face of limestone. So, there he was, standing up in the mid-upper gun turret with his camera, taking pictures. He kept telling Smithy our pilot, "Get closer, get closer." I'm sure we were only a few yards away from the cliffs.

We used to have some wild parties in the canteen. One day, a fellow came out of the canteen, which was on the second floor, fell down the stairs and broke his shoulder and hurt his leg and as a result he was declared "wounded in action." I cannot remember if he got posted home or not! We could just see his mother telling everyone about her poor son, who got injured in action, flying overseas on a bombing mission!

Ginger and I had decided to get married before being posted to an operational bombing squadron. Since I was only twenty years old, I had to wire my mother: "Please, send permission for me to get married". And it wasn't a shot gun wedding either! Since this meant that Ginger would be leaving Wales and her family after the war, her family was not too pleased with her getting married to an airman from the "Colonies" and I guess if a British girl married a Canadian, she would move far away and they may never see her again. In Britain, anyone from Canada, New Zealand, Australia or any of the so-called colonies, was considered a colonial. This attitude did not go over too well with most Canadians. Canada seemed very far away, because in those days, it meant a trip of ten days on the boat and another six days on the train. I think the British had heard a lot of different stories about us and the "Colonies" and I guess that they thought once she went that far away, they may never see her again.

I was never a church-going person. In preparing for the wedding, Ginger asked me: "Do you want to have the reading of the banns". I said, "Hell no, we just want a small wedding, why do we need a band?" I didn't know that "reading of the banns" was the notice to get married, to be read in the church, for three weeks in a row and was the same as getting a marriage license. I think you also needed a license but we did not have to pay for it, as her mother had the banns read. There wasn't too much specific training while at the conversion station as we concentrated getting used to a four-engine bomber by doing general flying and doing take off and landings. We were getting more general practice flying together as a crew. We were getting very close to the big thing, that is flying with a big load of bombs into Germany. Most

of our training focused on getting there and dropping the bombs, but getting back home was very important to us also. After the main excitement was over, Smithy used to say, "Getting off the ground with a full load of bombs, is half the trip." The next part of our training was a Commando course. We were all told that it would be tough, but it was a lot tougher than we were told. So Commando course, here we came. Three weeks of very tough training to get us ready in case we were shot down. Our duty was to avoid capture, keep as many Germans busy looking for us as possible, contact the Underground one way or the other and get back to England. The Commando course was run by the British Army and, as they were mostly regular army, they were real tough and wanted us to know it. They felt aircrew were real soft types and called us "Brylcream Boys" because of the popular Brylcream hair dressing of the time.

Fig.2b Lancaster Bomber

First, we were all reduced to privates, regardless of what rank we actually held. Although we had been in training for over a year, we had done very little physical work, having been either sitting in class, flying, or going on leave. On this course everything was done with a whistle, all on the double, no walking. We had to run all the time. No bicycles, no rides. They had us climbing ropes, running through ditches, over hills, through pipes, culverts, lots of mud and water. They wanted it to be like the real thing. They did a good job. I think they were in their glory, believe me, after a day of Commando training we sure slept at the end of the day and didn't go far from our barracks.

After the first week, they took us 12 miles into the country and dumped us off. We now had to get back to our base on our own, without using the roads or getting caught. Of course, they were out looking for us, and if we were found in a pub or on the road, they would take us back a few miles and we would have to start over again. If they found us in a taxi, they would get really angry and take us all the way back to the starting point.

At the end of the second week, we were taken twenty-five miles out, repeating the return to barracks all over again. Except now, we were in a bit better shape. By the end of the third week, it was the "big one." that is forty miles (which everyone talked about). We were instructed: "If you ever got shot down, you will have to walk a hell of a lot farther than that and you sure as hell can't use the roads." I guess all these things helped me later on but, as I mentioned before, I was about to get married. The big hike was on the Wednesday and the course would be over when we got back from the hike. However, I was to be married on the Saturday. It did not seem like a very good idea to go on the hike and I wanted to get out of it. There for I decided to go to the orderly room to see the Captain. I knew he was a tough miserable character but you never get what you do not ask for, especially in the armed forces. I explained to him, "Captain I am getting married on the weekend and as I do not feel a forty mile hike will help my honeymoon, I would like to get out of it". He said: "No way can I give you permission, but I'll tell you something your two week pass is already made up. It is in the top drawer of my desk and I am going for tea". The British always have their tea. I didn't say anything and it took me a few seconds to get what he was trying to tell me. Then it came to me. I saluted him and said, "Thank you Sir." I waited until he had gone for tea, took my pass, and off I went. I did not question him, and sure got out of there in a hurry!

I headed to Tredegar, in South Wales, where Ginger's family lived and where we were to be married. As soon as I got there we went to get our marriage license. Since we had to have it three days in advance. Everything went well, until the license clerk asked me for the Air Force permission to get married. I looked at him dumb. He said: "You have to have it as there have been too many servicemen getting married who were already married in Canada." We thought things over for a few minutes, then he said: "I will issue the license with today's date on it, but I cannot give it to you until you show me the permission". Things were not going to be that easy. I was suppose to be on the big forty mile hike. All my crew were on it. I phoned the orderly room and explained what I needed, but I did not tell them where I was. They told me they would make it up. Then I had to phone the squadron headquarters, to which my crew was returning and left a message for them to pick up the letter with the permission to get married. When they picked up their passes at the orderly room, my crew was supposed to let me know if they got it without any problems. When Saturday arrived, my big day to get married. All of my crew were coming there on Saturday morning. Bill Gardiner, my navigator, was going to be my best man. I had not heard a thing from them. I had stayed in a hotel in Tredegar on Friday night as it was supposed to be unlucky if you saw your bride after midnight before the wedding. I got up Saturday, not too bright and not that early. Ginger's father, brothers and brother-in-laws had taken me out on a stag party and I was never one to leave a party before it was over, especially if it was my last night of being single. I went down to the bus station to wait for my crew, worried about the permission. When the bus arrived they all clambered off, without a worry in their head. The guys had picked up the permission, but never thought of phoning me! We proceeded to grab a taxi and got the marriage license from the license office.

Fig.2c Ginger and I

The wedding was to take place in the Chapel. Ginger's Mother arrived late, since she had been attending to Ginger's wedding gown etc. I was waiting, already standing up in the front of the Church. With all my crew in the front row just behind me. Smithy, my pilot, kept whispering to me: "It's not too late, let's get the hell out of here." Then, he said to the crew: " I knew we stayed too long on that station; we should have got a posting before this thing got too serious." But before I could say any more, the organist started playing, "Here comes the bride". Ginger came down the aisle, wearing the most beautiful dress I had ever seen. In fact I hadn't known what she was going to wear. She wouldn't tell me. I don't think I had ever seen her in civilian clothes before, and she looked really different out of a uniform. We had the reception in the Mountain Inn pub across the road from Ginger's parents house. In Wales, a reception includes a lot of drinking beer and singing, so it was a very active day. Our honeymoon started immediately afterward with a bus ride of a few hours to the town of Gwent. The trip was memorable since, as we had rushed from the reception to the bus without a visit to the toilet, my kidneys almost burst. I survived, however, and we used up the rest of my two weeks leave wandering around that part of the country.

Fig.2d The full crew at my Wedding

We finished the trip back at Tredegar where I found Bill, my Navigator and best man, still there, as he had developed a great liking for Wales. On my return from my honeymoon, I found we were off to

Yorkshire to convert to Halifax bombers, the main four-engine aircraft used by No. 6 Group's squadrons. Up to now, we had been flying two-engine aircraft, Ansons and Whitneys. Much of the training with our larger aircraft consisted of doing "Circuits and Bumps", which were take-offs and landings. This include landing with three engines and flying with two or three engines to help prepare us in case we were damaged while on a bombing run over Germany. 419 Squadron was based in Yorkshire, near a small town called Middleton St. George. The Squadron was called the "Moose Squadron" after Dave "Moose" Fulton from Kamloops BC, the squadron's original commanding officer. The City of Kamloops was our squadron sponsor and it still is to this date. Dave Fulton was always talking about moose, so he was nick-named: "Moose Fulton". He had been shot down before I arrived at the squadron and he never made it back. "Moosa Aswayita", the squadron motto, means "Beware of The Moose." On August 11, 1944, the King of England officially presented the moose emblem to 419 Squadron. This Squadron became the most decorated unit in the RCAF during World War II and is now based in Cold, Lake Alberta.

We were a very close crew by now, having flown together since we first met back in Honeybourne, seven months previously. We only flew once with another pilot and, during this flight were diverted to a station in southern England because of bad weather. As a result of this, it took us a week to finally get back to our home Squadron. We had landed in Linton, where, because of the heavy rains, the dirt runway had become too soft for our heavy bomber to take off. As Linton was a test squadron, all the air crew were officers. Our crew, however, were all NCO's so we had a ball in their mess and got very spoiled by the WAF's (Women Auxiliary Air Force).

On our way home we had to go through London to get back to our squadron from Linton. There, people stared at us as we were still wearing our flying suits and carrying our parachutes. We had signed them out so we were responsible for them. I think a lot of people thought we had crashed some place and were walking home! It was always considered bad luck if we flew with another crew. But then again, my friend Bill Ritchie lost his crew during the first part of his tour when he was sick, and his crew flew without him.

They got shot down but he completed his tour of operations as a spare Bomb Aimer, having a different crew every night he flew. Whenever a Bomb Aimer in another crew was sick or could not fly, he substituted for them. He is now living happily in Virden, Manitoba. Our operational bombing mission started on a particular night, and followed a certain pattern which we soon got used to. The day preceding a night bombing mission was filled with a schedule of tasks which we routinely followed. If it was "go" for our crew, we would have to go to the Dispersal Area, where our aircraft was kept. They were put in small groups all around the airfield. They would never keep too many planes in one place in case we were bombed. There would be a truck to take us out to our plane.

Fig.2e Lancaster in flight

The gunners would check their turrets and the guns, making sure they were working perfectly and had plenty of ammunition. I would examine the camera and the bomb sights, and verify the front turret, the guns and shells. The navigator would look at his instruments and his radar, (such as it was in those days). It was my job to plot our position. I always liked to use the star Betelgeuse, in the constellation Orio. The wireless air gunner would test his radio. The pilot would verify all his controls and the plane in general. The engineer would examine the controls and the different things to do with the engines. The ground crew did a great job of keeping the plane in shape, but it was our neck up there, not theirs. Once we had taken off, it was too late to complain. We were all posted from there, some to become Instructors and they seemed very happy, although I would have hated it. Often the trip would be cancelled. When it wasn't the weather, it was sometimes intelligence that had found out something at the last minute.

Fig.2f My crew's picture taken by me on Squadron

Each trip had special bombs matched to whatever target we were going after. The next thing we had to do was go check out our parachute. There was no way of testing that. You had to have full faith in the group that were packing them. The big joke around the parachute depot was: "If it does not work, bring it back, we will give you your money back!" About 2 p.m. we would start our briefing. All the crews would be there. The Commanding Officer would give us a few words of encouragement to the assembled crews, telling us the importance of this particular bombing raid. All the raids were (all very important).

Fig.2g A big one, on the 1,000 sortie.

Then, he would take the cover off the large map on the wall, show us where our target was for that night, and tell us what we were going after.

There was generally lots of "ahs" of one kind or another. If it was a short trip or not in to the Ruhr we would all say: "A piece of cake". However, if it was in the Ruhr, we would all say, "ah" because the Ruhr was always a very hot target. A lot of flak from the anti-aircraft guns would be fired at us, exploding at a given height. Generally, the German gunners tried to guess what height we were flying and just keep pumping the flak at us. They also had big search-lights which they kept moving around the sky. If you got caught in one, you had to get out of the cone of light before the gunners down below spotted you and locked their guns on you. To get out of the search-lights, the pilot would have to corkscrew, diving to the right and then up to the left. There was generally many of our own bombers around, so you had to watch very carefully not to collide with one.

The Germans always had lots of fighters defending the Ruhr, because that was where their main steel factories and a number of their ammunition manufacturing was located. Everyone looked out for fighters. We would first see them when they were just a spot in the sky. They flew very fast, if they saw you first, they were after you. The gunners went into full swing and the pilot would start to corkscrew. It could be a very busy night.

If the trip was to Berlin, that was going to be very exciting, as this city was very well protected, with lots of flak and searchlights. Most of their fighter aircraft were there or in the Ruhr. Because it was a long trip, we would take "Wakey Wakey" pills, as we called them, to keep us from falling asleep. Later, when we got back and finished the interrogations, which would be early in the morning, we would then take sleeping pills to go to sleep.

The Navigation Leader would then give a talk on the flight times to the points where we were to be at certain times and the exact time to be over the target. It was very important that we all stayed together. If you got behind or strayed off course, a fighter plane could easily pick you off. The Navigator Leader gave out all the maps of the area we would be flying over and described the navigation aids that may be available. We would be given the exact height to fly with stacks of bombers arranged 1000 feet apart vertically.

The meteorological officer would tell us what weather to expect, where winds were blowing from and how strong they were, both of which had a great affect on our navigation. He also forecast the cloud cover. The worst conditions that we anticipated, would be a full moon without clouds in the sky for cover. We were up there, like clay pigeons, for the Germans to shoot at. But, if you cannot see the stars, you can't navigate with them and then you have to depend on your radar, which wasn't too good in those days. The meteorologists had a hard time, to give us the exact weather as they had very few reports on the weather far to the east. But, I guess, in general, their forecasts were reasonable. One night, for example, we were flying deep, into Germany. They told us that we would have cloud cover all the way, but it was as clear as a bell with a full moon. That was a very scary night, but we were very lucky as there weren't many fighters around.

The Bombing Squadron Leader would familiarise us with the type of bombs that we were going to drop, tell us what our code name would be and advise us what the Pathfinders were going to drop over the target. The Pathfinders were a squadron of highly experienced flyers who mostly flew Mosquito aircraft, a fast two-engine fighter bomber. They flew very low over the target and dropped different coloured marker flares, showing us where to bomb. They would keep changing the selected colour and moving the aiming point. If our code name was "Daisy", the Pathfinder would call out: "Daisy hit the red! Hit the red!" Then later they would change colour and say:

"Daisy hit the green! Hit the green!" Everything would be lit up like a Christmas Tree. As the target got hotter with more flak and more fighters, they would shout out, "for God's sake, you guys, let's get going! We have to get home tonight Bomb on the blue! Bomb on the blue!" The role of the Pathfinder was very dangerous as the Germans were shooting at them from the ground and we were dropping bombs around them from above.

The Intelligence Officer would tell us various things such as what the Underground was doing and what area we were flying over. He would give us our escape kit, in case we got shot down. They consisted of maps, printed on silk, of the area that we were flying over and a chart of the different languages that we might run. We were taught phrases such as: "I am British, can you hide me?" or "Can you give me something to eat?" We also received a package of the various currencies for each country, a few chocolate bars for energy and concentrated foods to last a couple of days. We did not take these things very seriously as it was always going to be the other guy who got shot down, not us. We were told it was our duty to escape if we got shot down and we were to do our best to get back to England. If we were captured, we were to try and escape again and to keep as many Germans busy looking for us as possible. The more Germans we kept busy, the less manpower they had in the front line.

The Gunnery Officers would give us an idea of what we could expect from the German fighter planes. They would have all the reports from the last flight over that area based on information gathered from crews returning from previous bombing trips. Generally, the planes went to one or two targets, but at times a smaller group would head to another area ahead of the main bombing group, to confuse the fighter defence. Many times the Germans would try new tactics and we would be told of these tricks.

Following these briefings, we would then split up into separate groups. That is, the pilots, navigators, bomb aimers, wireless air gunners and engineers would each go over everything in more detail. There was a lot of work and detail to a bombing run. We had been trained for over eighteen months, flying a plane worth hundreds of thousands of dollars, and our own lives were at stake. Often a whole crew, with a brand new plane, would go down the first night. The statistics of the a crew lasting a full tour of "Ops" weren't too good. We always felt it would be the other crew that got shot down.

After all this preparations, it would be time for dinner. Since air crew were always treated well. It was always a custom to give us eggs and sometime steak before a bombing run. After we ate, we would get our flying gear on and report to the squadron room. A truck would then pick us up and take us out to the aircraft where we would make all our final preparations. Everyone would usually be tense and excited, joking with each other and with the other crews. As the bombs were being loaded in the bomb bays, we would use chalk paint to write different words on the bombs. Sometimes we would blow up condoms, and tie them on the end of the bombs. Our Wireless Air

Gunner was a Catholic and this embarrassed him a lot, as the Padre would come around to the plane before we took off to wish us good luck. They would hand out candies and "Wakey Wakey" pills. These pills were often necessary by the time we got home. We would have often been on the go for maybe eighteen hours and, with the high altitude, the tension of the situation and the drum of the motors, we were very tired by the end of the op.

It was always a long drag returning home, across the Channel, back to base, sometimes circling the base for an hour or so, waiting for our turn to land. Often a plane would come in, having been hit, with engine trouble, or low on gas. If that happened you had to let it land ahead of you. About the worst that could happen on your return was for your airfield to be fogged in and have to go to another base which was clear. After landing you would have to taxi to your dispersal area and your ground crew would be waiting for you. They had to tie the plane down, check for any damage or any mechanical trouble and then fully service the plane, making it ready for the next day. The ground crew were very proud of their plane so they looked after them very carefully. Every aircraft that could fly had to be up in the air. If not, someone had to give a good reason why.

With our aircraft, we had to wait for a truck to pick us up and take us to the Squadron Room where tea or horrible English coffee with a bun or cookie would be waiting. Then we had to take our turn to be debriefed! All the Squadron Leaders would be there. We had to report everything that happened or did not happen, what we saw on the way there and the way back, and what happened over the target. Did we hit what we were after? of course they had the pictures the next day from the cameras connected to our bomb sights, which showed where our bombs fell. We would report any planes we saw shot down and where we saw them. Did we see any parachutes open up? How many fighters were there? How much flak did we see? Where was the flak? If there was a lot of flak, was it all in one place? If so they would send some fast bombers over, to try to knock it out. But in most case, the German anti-aircraft guns were positioned on railway cars or trucks and would keep moving so they could not be pinpointed. We also had to put in a report on the mechanical workings of our plane. We would be very tired by now but we all would wait around to make sure everyone got back. Sometimes one of our planes would have to land at another field for some reason, but they would get in touch with the squadron and let us know. We would then head for the mess to eat where we always got a big plate of ham and eggs; plus a steak sometimes. That was the tradition. Then off to bed, with generally a sleeping pill, and God protect anyone that disturbed us! We still did a lot of training flights all over England.

Fig.2h Lancasters on the Runway, ready for take off

There was always something one of us was weak on, or something new which needed learning. However, a lot of the time England was covered with low clouds so it was kind of nice to go above the clouds and fly in the sunshine.

We were all very practical about what happened to the personal things of anyone who got shot down. Jack Friday and I had a deal that, if one of us got shot down, the other would take the missing man's cigarettes and goodies. Jack Friday was always a good one with which to make this agreement because his father owned a drug store and would always send him licorice and other candies. If you went missing, those things were neither sent home nor kept until you got back. They wouldn't keep. So, I got Jack's articles, but then someone else got mine.

On the Squadron base, we lived in Nissen huts curved metal buildings, very bare and cold. They were scattered around in little groups with a semi-closed washroom in the middle, called the ablutions, with no glass in the windows. The British who designed these were very hardy people! Many times there was little or no hot water, so you wasted no time doing whatever you went there to do. Each crew lived in one hut, heated on a little stove in the middle that burned coke, of which you could get a bucket every few days. That was from November to May. If it was a cool Spring, that was too bad. Then we would steal farmer's fences or anything else that would burn. When the guards were not on duty, we 'liberated' coke from the coke shed.

Our beds were little cots with a spring hung like a hammock from a metal frame. Instead of a mattress, we had three cushions about two feet square, called "biscuits". I never found out why they were made that way. If you were a Private (or I guess ground crew), you had to take your bed apart and pile your "biscuits" at the end of your bed with your blankets carefully folded on top. We, as air crew, never did this ceremony. We never made our beds, except on the day we had our sheets changed, which was weekly. I guess if we had made our beds every day we would have had a more comfortable sleep. We would often sleep in our flying suits to keep warm.

Being in Bomber Command was dangerous not only when flying over enemy territory but from the moment the bombs were loaded on the tarmac. One night we were sitting on the tarmac, the area where the aircraft lined up before take off. One of the crews, who we knew very well, got to the end of the runway taking off and something happened. They blew up in front of us! The control tower flashed the red light, stopping everything for a very short time. They changed runways and started flashing the green light for take off, not giving us time to think about it. You could not dwell on things like that, or you might get nervous about what you were doing. Strangely, I can't think now who it was that crashed that night on the runway.

In the Spring of 1944, we began our operational missions with short-range missions into western France but by March we were flying deeper into Germany. The target for our first bombing run was a railway yard in Ghent, Belgium where the Germans had a large marshalling yard. It was a little frightening as it was our first major target, but we were "eager beavers". There wasn't very much flak and not too many fighter planes. We just nipped across the Channel into Belgium and out again.

Our second flight was to Boulogne, France. W e met a lot of flak and fighters over the target and ran into a thunderstorm on our way back. Smithy was stretching his legs and wanted to go back to see what it was like at the gunners station. "I was flying the plane" when suddenly the aerial around the plane was lit up like a neon sign. We were bouncing all over the place. We were flying over the English Channel and generally considered ourselves safe as we were almost home. The odd time a German fighter would follow us, knowing we would be off guard, then attack us. But this time all went well. Smithy came back to the controls and he flew back to base.

One night when we came back there was no visibility because of heavy fog over Yorkshire. We were trying to land and missed the runway a little. I looked out the window and could see the barracks right next to us. We sure pulled up and got out of there in a hurry, we all hollering at Smithy. We got back in the circuit again, but it was too foggy to land at home base, so we finally landed at another station and went back to the squadron in the morning.

D-day, the 6th of June, was a very exciting night. Everything that could fly was up in the air bombing everywhere, trying to keep the Germans in suspense. We drew the late shift and took off very late at night to bomb Coutance in Normandy. It was a cloudy night and we could not see much of what was going on down below. Every once in a while the clouds would break and we would see all the boats down below. We were night bombers but it was almost dawn when we started for home and, by then, we could see all the American day bombers getting into the air. There were so many planes in the air we had to land at a base in Southern England, called Colerne. After we had a little sleep and had breakfast, we were sent back to our squadron for debriefing.

A few days after D- Day, the Army was having trouble with one particular area which we had to bomb at low level. It was a bright night and we were following the railway lines. We found our target and bombed it, but we were flying so low that, when the bombs hit, the concussion blew us straight up in the air. It scared the hell out of us because we were not expecting it and we didn't know what had hit us. W e got back on track and got home safely. I thing we all were a little scared that night, we all peed our pants a little.

The Americans flew Flying Fortresses which had a lot of armour and fighter planes flying escort. They would fly in a group and bomb in a group. We flew in a group, sometimes as many as 500 bombers, but each plane was totally on its own. We did our own navigating, found the target and bombed the target all on our own. Sometimes we would not see another aircraft, but we knew they were all around; above us, below us or, at either side. Sometimes over the target, when everything was lit up like a Christmas tree, we could clearly see the planes below us, but had to watch for the planes above us. We didn't want them to drop their bombs on us.

Chapter Three

June Sixteenth to Rakers

The most important night of the war, for me, began on June 16, 1944. This was our ninth bombing trip
over Germany and we were all feeling confident! All
our trips so far had been a piece of cake. We had returned, to base safely each time despite running into
fighters and flak. Quite a few of my friends, however,
had been shot down or were missing. We didn't know
if they had been killed, made prisoner of war (POW)
or were running on the loose. We were all so sure it
would never happen to us. It was always going to be
the other crew that got shot down, or as we would say,
"get the chop".

Ten days had passed since D-Day. June 16 was
not a nice day rainy and very overcast. Our name was
up on the squadron reports. We didn't know where
we were going, but we figured we would just nip over
and back. I was writing a letter to Ginger but never
got it finished, thinking that I would finish it when I
got back. Bill Gardiner wrote a letter to his wife (he
always wrote her before we took off) and gave it to me

to mail on my way up to headquarters, but I forgot to mail it. I never told him before we took off.

As usual we didn't know where we were going. W e wouldn't know until the briefing as the mission was always kept very secret. As they always said, "One never knew when the enemy was listening." We went to briefing and were told that, despite a poor weather forecast, we were going to Sterkrade, a synthetic oil refinery in the Ruhr. "The Germans had this site very well protected and we were told to expect heavy flak. As there was a fighter squadron base very close by, we could also expect a lot of German interceptors." The oil refinery was a very important target. The oil was badly needed for their war effort and their main steel mills and manufacturing plants were all around this area.

The first briefing included everyone and covered all aspects of the mission where we were going and what to expect. We were then split up into our different groups, such as pilots, navigators, bomb aimers, gunners etc., when we got specific information according to our trade. We got our briefing material, bomb load, weather report, maps, escape kits, and pep talk. We were told to expect cloud cover.

We then had the special dinner that we always got sort of a farewell dinner. Air crew always had their ham and eggs before a trip, the same as when they returned that was tradition, like the Navy with their shot of rum. Then we picked up our parachutes. The people who folded our parachutes always told us the same thing: "If it doesn't open, bring it back and we will give you another one!" Then we headed down to the dispersal site to our aircraft. We always went by truck because when we have our full flying gear on and carrying your parachute, you didn't want to walk too far.

Everyone was in good spirits, (because we were making our first trip to the Ruhr,) our bomb load was very special. We wrote silly things on the bombs with chalk and attached inflated condoms. Our Wireless Air Gunner of course was very embarrassed when the priest came around to give us a few words of encouragement as well as chocolate, gum and our wake-up pills. The rest of us, being very young, did not care.

Sometimes it was a very long night. We would start at noon, checking the aircraft, have our briefing, have dinner, take off at dusk or 7 or 8 o'clock and back home at 3 or 4 o'clock in the morning. Some members of our crew, like our navigator, Bill Gardiner, got air sickness pills. It was awful to see poor Gardy. He had a bucket next to him that he would vomit in, wipe his face off with his sleeve and keep on working. He was sick almost every time. A navigator was very busy keeping track of where we were. There would be hundreds of planes up there at the same time and we would want to keep right in the middle. If one strayed out of the group, a fighter would get you or the ground defences could get you in their searchlights and "bingo" you were gone. It was the testing of air sick pills on the air crew through the war, that made the "car sick" pill "Gravol" as we know it today.

While awaiting take off, we passed some time by kibitzing with some of the other crews watching a farmer just over the fence working in the field as it was getting dusk, we all agreed we were better off flying than working in the field from morning to night. We got the signal to start our engines, to do the final tests, and get ready to taxi into our proper position. We were all organised and lined up at the end of the runway, each plane in its place ready for take off. W e began to be a little tense, waiting to see the green light flashing telling us to take off because some times the trip would be scrubbed at the last minute, because of weather or something intelligence knew, but "they never told us why."

We took off just before dark as it would take a couple of hours to get to our height and get over the coast. We had one 4,000 lb. and twelve 500 lb. bombs, considered to be a big bomb load at that time. Smithy always said: "Getting off the ground with a full load of bombs is a big part of the trip." There would be seven or eight bombers taking off from each squadron which were scattered all over Yorkshire. On this bombing raid there were 321 Lancaster and Halifax bombers and twelve Mosquitoes from No 1, No 4, No 6, and No 8 Bombing Group. We would all be making big circles and slowly heading for the coast. W e would have the exact times to be in a certain place so we would be all together in a group. When there was a big group of us we would drop tin foil to fool their radar. It would be like one big blur on their screen and they would just shoot up in the sky hoping to hit something. All our crews were on their own, as it was very dark, so the navigators had to be very exact. There would be hundreds of us at different heights but we would often not see anyone except over the target when everything was lit up. Everything came to life over the target because of the searchlights, flak and fires.

The Germans had another device that would scare the hell out of us and put us on edge. They would send a balloon up in the air, and explode it making a lot of noise with bursting bright lights, and you wouldn't know where it was coming from or where it was going.

We did not expected too much fighter activity as another big raid, with 405 Lancasters and Halifaxes, was to attack German flying bomb launching sites in the Pas-de-Calais, earlier. We hoped the German fighters would all be going down there after them. It was quiet most of the way to our target, but then all hell broke loose and we started to get flak from everywhere. It was very cloudy down below with lots of cloud cover, so they were pumping the flak everywhere. They were not kidding us when they said: "there will be lots of flak." It was coming from everywhere. Talk about a fireworks display! It would have been nice to see, if they were not so damn serious about hitting us. The gunners got some good practice in. We started dropping a lot of tin foil and were on edge, watching for anything that may be coming at us, just like when you disturb a hornets nest. Suddenly we heard Sid, our tail gunner, very excited: "Have a Jerry fighter at one o'clock." We could hear the rattle of machine gun. Next, we heard Sid call out: "Cork-screw hard and fast". When you are corkscrewing you have to watch carefully for other aircraft as we knew there were 321 of our own planes very close by. Smithy swung the aircraft hard, to the right and down, and then to the left and up. If you think the giant dipper is something you should try this. Unfortunately, I never did like the giant dipper. He repeated this three times and we lost the fighter.

On the final bomb run into the target, my job was to lay down in the front of the aircraft, checking over the bomb sight, and putting the final setting in. There were a lot of variants to enter, such as our speed, the height we were flying, our direction and speed and direction of the wind. I had to get the latest reading from the navigator and the exact speed from the pilot, all the while watching out for German fighter planes. We also had to watch out for our own planes both below us and above us. We didn't want to be hit by their bombs and didn't want to be bomb any aircraft below us. The flak, bursting right in front of us, seemed to be a half a mile or so ahead of us and exploding at the same height that we were flying. I said to Smithy, "did you see that?" he said, "hell man, I am looking right at it."

When we got over the target, the flak was just below us, so it didn't present a danger to us. As we started on the bombing run, we knew there were lots of planes above us and below us. At this point we began to see some of them. It seemed funny how we could fly for hours and not see anyone until arriving right over the target. Then all the lights down below started flashing and the flak lit up the sky. With over three hundred bombers on this raid, there were a lot of bombers over one spot about the same time, all stacked up every thousand feet, all converging on the same target. As a result, we had to hope for the best that we wouldn't get hit by the flak or the fighters and, at the same time, watch for the planes above us dropping their bombs. This mission was one of the worst we had experienced.

The bombing this night didn't turn out very well. The whole target area was covered with a thin layer of clouds and the markers soon disappeared. So we had to bomb on the glow seen through the clouds. As we left the target, the bombs were exploding, the flak was everywhere, and the sky was lit up like the "Fourth of July." Twenty bombers were shot down that night. We were glad to get away from the target area and head back home. When our bombs were dropped, the biggest part of the trip was over and we, as usual on the return leg, felt relieved. As we were heading home, however, we flew near the German night fighter beacon at Bocholt which the Germans used as their holding airdrome for their night fighters. We were hoping they had all left for where our other bombers were. Again, all hell broke loose. Sid was on the intercom, "Fighter on our tail, at six o'clock, cork-screw, cork-screw," and all our guns were blazing. Smithy could manipulate the plane a little faster now as we had dropped our bombs and the plane was a lot lighter. We had a fighter on our tail twice before we finally left the area.

After throwing off these fighters, things got quieter. We were away from the target, going across Holland, on our way home. I guess the fighters were chasing someone else instead of us. There was the odd bit of flak coming up, but they were only shooting into the air hoping to hit something as we had good cloud cover. Most of it seemed to be over. A couple of more legs and we would be across the channel and down to base. I could see the coast on the radar screen and started helping Gardy get a good fix on it as we had corkscrewed around so much we were not sure that we were on track. I took a couple of shots with the sextant on my favourite star Betelgeuse. (It was always my favourite because I could always find it. There are a lot of stars up there so you had best use one you can easily identify!)

All of a sudden, out of the blue, Bill Baran, the WAG called out "there is a fire in the fuselage." That was a surprise because we hadn't felt anything. I grabbed the fire extinguisher and headed for the centre of the plane, but it was too late. It was already a mass of flame. The oxygen lines must have been fuelling the fire and there was no way it could be put out. When I reported that it was too big to put out, Smithy called out on the intercom, "Abandon Aircraft. Abandon Aircraft!".

It was surprising that we were all quite calm. The engineer headed to the nose of the plane to open the escape hatch, through which we all had to get out, except for the gunners they could go out through their turrets. I found my parachute and got it on (we were generally a little careless where we put them, really not expecting to have to use them). I went to the nose to get ready to jump. However, when the engineer had opened the escape door, instead of pulling it in to the nose of the aircraft, he tried to push it out and the slipstream jammed the door, now it couldn't be moved. We had been taught a hundred times: "Pick up the door and bring it in the aircraft." By now, we were both struggling with the door, Bill our navigator, was pushing me, and the rest of the crew pushing him, wondering what was the matter. It was very black and our intercom was not on. Meanwhile, the fire was getting worse and was all around us. We all started to get panicky. I had pulled off my oxygen mask when I went back to the fire and was close to passing out with the lack of oxygen. The last thing I remember was the fire. Then all hell broke loose. Everything blew. I guess the gas tanks exploded. I can remember being thrown all over the place, tossed from one side of the aircraft to the other and I really believed the end had come. I regretted that I never had time to say good-bye to my mother or Ginger. I was knocked unconscious or I might have just passed out with the lack of oxygen, as we were flying at 21,000 feet, when the fire started. The usual procedure is to put oxygen masks on at 10,000 feet altitude.

I don't know what happened to Glen and Mike who were our tail and mid-upper gunners. I don't imagine they could hear us on the intercom as the intercom-wire to them was more than likely burned when the fire first started. I imagine Smithy was behind Bill Gardiner and Mike Baran behind him. I guess when the plane exploded, we all went sky high. I found out after the war that two of the crew never got out of the plane and were carbonised. The engineer who was flying with us was picked up by the Germans. The others had not even pulled the handle on their chutes; two were reduced to ashes and still in the plane and three were found dead on the ground.

I hadn't believed in miracles until I woke up, free falling through the air, with no chute. I could see the aircraft burning in the distance, pieces falling all around me, I was all alone. I mean all alone. I felt on my chest for my parachute (we wore the RAF observer-type parachute that strapped on the chest pack) to pull the rip cord but it wasn't there. That gave me a horrible shock. Then, I could feel a bit of a pull, so I reached up above my head and found that the pack had been unhooked from my chest and had swung above my head. I have had enough presence of mind to reach up and pull the rip cord to open it. I pulled the cord and slowed down with a very big jerk. I can't remember if I protected my privates or not! With parachutes, the straps come around, through the top of your legs, and one's privates can get damaged very easily. There are certain parts of one's body a person has to look after. But all seemed to work out all right.

The night was black, raining like hell, and pieces of the aircraft were falling around me. I felt all alone in the world! I couldn't see anything except the aircraft burning in the distance. I didn't know how high I was but I knew I would not have had enough oxygen to come to until around ten thousand feet. So, I must have been somewhere below ten thousand feet and the ground. I didn't know when I was going to hit the ground. I was always afraid of landing on a Church steeple. I must have seen that in a movie or somewhere . So many things were going through my mind.

Was I going to be prisoner of war? Would I land in water? In a town? In the bush? On a roof? Or in the street? What sort of people would I meet? Could I get in touch with the Dutch Underground? I tried to keep my legs relaxed, in a crouched position, ready to land in or on whatever. The darkness and the rain were so very black!

I didn't have to wait long for my questions to be answered. I figured that I must have been at a few thousand feet when I opened my parachute because I was suddenly falling through branches! My parachute got hung up in a tree and there I was swinging in the branches and the breeze. It was still pitch black and I couldn't see a thing. I couldn't even see the ground. I imagined that I was just a few feet from the ground. I could hear dogs barking for miles. I could also imagine the Germans chasing and looking for me with their dogs. Without thinking too much, I pulled myself up, using my parachute lines, to release the pressure. I then released my harness and bang!!! I went all the way down, not one or two feet as I had guessed, but 10 or 15 feet. It gave me quite a shock. I hurt my knee, scratched the skin off my left arm and my right shoulder was a little sprained and very sore. I hurt all over, either from the fire, from the plane exploding, or from the fall. But there I was, sitting on the ground, pinching myself to make sure I wasn't having a bad dream. Was I really in Holland all alone? I knew that some crews that crash landed in England thought they were in enemy territory. One thing I was sure of was that I did not want to be a prisoner of war. I then had to get serious and do something.

It was so dark and wet, I couldn't see my parachute above or I didn't think of it. I first took off my "Mae-West", the life vest that we wore all the time in case we landed in water. I tried to bury it with some personal things that I had in my pocket, things I didn't want the Germans to see, in case I got caught. I also had the letter that my navigator had written to his wife, which I was supposed to have mailed on our way to the Mess Hall. I tried to dig a hole but I ended up covering it only with moss, leaves and stuff. W e were trained to do this so the Germans wouldn't know exactly where we landed. I didn't think about my parachute still flying in the tree, visible for miles. I did not have a gun with me as I never liked them. Also, I could not imagine myself with a little hand gun running into a bunch of Germans with machine guns. Then it would be good night for ever. We carried two escape packages: one with very concentrated food (milk chocolate, vitamins, pills to purify water, etc.); the other with maps of all the European countries that we were going to fly over (Germany, Belgium, France and Holland). They were printed on silk so it didn't matter if they got wet. There was also money for each country. I was lucky to have these with me a s often we were not careful where we kept them when we were flying since we were not planning to get shot down. That was supposed to happen to the other fellows. I must have grabbed mine before all hell broke loose. My first thought was to get away from where I was and away from the crash. I tore all the badges off my jacket hoping to look as inconspicuous as possible, then I started walking, guessing south by instinct. I had a small compass in my pocket and one of my buttons was a compass, but it was too dark to use them. I came to a big fence which I couldn't climb over. I was thinking that maybe I was in a military area or maybe there was one on the other side of the fence. It was very hard walking in heavy bush. I didn't see anything until I hit it. So I went the other way. I continued to hear dogs barking all around and I felt they were all looking for me. I walked for about an hour, becoming pretty wet and miserable.

Fig.3a For me "The war is over"

Occasionally, I thought I heard someone talking, would stand still for a while, but then I wouldn't hear anything. I wondered if it might be one of my crew or be someone looking for me. The dogs seemed to have gotten closer. I thought the Germans might have had dogs out for me so I climbed a tree and stayed there for quite a while. I found out later that I had landed very close to a large dog kennel.

I continued to walk south, figuring the Allied lines were somewhere in that direction, and hoping that someone would hide me or help me go south. Eventually, I came to a main road but didn't want to cross it. I walked up the side of it for a while until I saw an outline of a church and, deciding I was in a town, started heading the other way. After walking for a while I decided it was too dangerous to continue to walk until day break. I knew there was a curfew and anyone walking at night would be picked up or shot. So I lay down under a tree and tried to rest. The rain was coming down pretty hard, however, and I found you can't rest very much with the rain falling on your face. So I just sat! It was too dark to look at my maps so I checked through my pockets, again, to make sure there was nothing in them that would give the Germans any information if I was captured. The time went slowly but daylight finally came. As soon as it was light enough to see, I got out my maps to try to figure out where I was.

I knew we were near Utrecht before we crashed so I found it on the map. I believed I had a good knowledge of geography, but could not think what language was spoken in this part of Europe. From a foreign language phrase book we carried, I looked up Dutch and memorised, "I am English, can you hide me." I decided to go south into France where our troops had landed. Although I did not realise the distance, I had my small compass and started on my way. My leg was sore, I felt like hell, but I knew I had to keep moving and try to get in touch with the Underground. We had been briefed on the Underground and given a few ideas of how to contact them. We were told to look for a young fellow on a lonely road and to make sure he was alone. If he was a German, or a German sympathiser, there was a 50/50 chance you could get away from him. Or we were to go to a small farm house without a telephone. With this in mind, I lay in the ditch by this small road until a fellow came along on a bicycle. I then motioned to him to come over and spoke to him, in what I thought was good Dutch according to the piece of paper I had. He didn't seem to know that I was trying to say, "I am English and can you hide me." I think he knew I was English but he seemed afraid to help me. He motioned me to go the other way as the Germans were up the way he was going. So I started to walk the other way.

I walked through bushes, and along the lanes and the trails for an hour or so. I saw a few German soldiers whose uniforms were much the same colour as mine. I had taken off my wings, Canadian badges and stripes, so I felt relatively safe. I decided to walk as if I was supposed to be there instead of sneaking around, thinking I might not be noticed so much. W e didn't have much practice at this in England. Coming to a little farm house, I went to the back door and said, in what I thought was good Dutch, "I am English, can you hide me." The occupants couldn't understand me, so I showed them on the paper what I was trying to say. They were old people however, and were afraid to help me. They gave me a piece of bread with something on it. It tasted horrible but I ate it because I knew I would need the energy. Before I had finished the bread, I moved away from the house, in case they called the Germans, and sat by a road again. I then saw some girls in uniforms going by. They looked young so I thought they might be school girls from some private school. Fortunately for me, I did not stop them. I found out later that they were German Army girls so I don't think they would have had much pity for me. I waited around for a while longer, sitting in the ditch, waiting for an opportunity to talk to someone. A while later, a young man on a bicycle came along. Because he had a leather briefcase on the carrier on the back of his bike, I thought maybe he was a student or a teacher so I took my chance. I called out and waved him over to me, as I was a little afraid to go out onto the road.

Fig.3b Frits the man that picked me up. Died Aug. 1987

He stopped and said something in Dutch. I didn't know what he said but I replied in my Dutch: "I am English, can you hide me?" He didn't have the least idea what I said as my pronunciation hadn't improved. I showed him my wings, said "RAF" and pointed to the sky. His face lit up and he asked me in perfect English, "are you Tommy?" I said "yes." What a relief that he spoke English! He asked me some pointed questions. Was I alone? Where did I crash? Where was my crew ? I answered these and showed him everything, trying to prove that I was English.

The Dutch had to be very careful as the Gestapo and Secret State Police (Geheimedienst) also dressed in Allied uniforms, and then they tried to make contact with the Underground. "If an Underground group was infiltrated, all members would be arrested and shot by the Germans."

So there we were, he wasn't that sure of me and I didn't know if he was sincere or just taking me to the Germans. But we took a chance on each other. He told me to sit on the back of his bicycle and we rode off down the road from the town of Siesta to Driebergen, along the Arnhemse Bovenweg. We soon came to a small corner store in this small village of the name of Zeist, at 95 Loolaan Street. I was now getting a little nervous because I was still wearing my uniform which had a torn arm and was a little burnt. My face and hair were the same. I was really sweating it out. It was very hard to know if he was on my side or not, but I didn't have many other options.

Fig.3c Mr. and Mrs. Bos' store that I was first taken to

When we arrived at the little corner store, he stopped at the curb and told me to wait there a minute. He left me holding his bicycle and went inside. Just as he left, two German soldiers came walking down the road. They looked at me, nodded, I nodded back and they kept on walking. But as I said before, the average German uniform was very similar to mine. If a couple of our privates saw a German in his uniform with everything cut off he might not have thought anything about it either. But standing there looking at his big red arm band with a big swastika on it. I fully realised then that I wasn't just dreaming, that I was not in the local theatre watching a movie. This was the real thing and I was in it! The fellow came out in a few minutes, said, "the coast is clear," and took me into the store.

I later found out that the fellow who picked me up was called "Frits" and was one of the important men in the Underground. Inside, I met Mr. and Mrs. Bos, the owners of the store. They asked me a few questions on different things. I had a few cigarettes so I gave them those along with a couple of pieces of chocolate in my pocket. The chocolate had melted and was a bit dirty, but they thought it was delicious. They had never seen chocolate since the Germans took over.

The Bos' family welcomed me without hesitation and did everything they could to make me comfortable. When they realised my left arm had been badly scratched, they became concerned and applied some first aid by pouring iodine on the arm. It caused quite a tingle, but of course only for a minute. "Mrs. Bos had a tear in her eye and said to her son, "such a young boy and his poor mother, how she must be worrying."

We talked for a while and then had something to eat: a bowl of hot porridge and bread, not black but almost, and I had my first Dutch cigar which they claimed was nothing like peacetime. I believed them. After that I was taken upstairs to wash and change. I put on some dry civilian clothes and dry underwear. The fresh clothes really felt wonderful, even though they didn't fit. I was going to lay down for a while but three men arrived and began to ask me a lot more questions. One was the store owner's son, nicknamed "The Teacher" as he could speak English and was actually teacher.

Fig.3d The Bos' family who owned the store

He was the main interrogator and I learned later that his name was Eep Bos. He told me later all he could think of was how a young boy like me could survive in Holland, he is so young and cannot speak a word of Dutch. They wanted to know about England, how things were there and when I figured the war would be over. They asked my name, number and where I was from, and said a few insulting things in German. They later told me that I would have surely reacted to the insults if I had been German. All kinds of questions on Canada, England, the war and what was going on in general so they could radio back to London to check on me. They were taking a big chance and wanted to be sure. They had secret radios and were in contact with intelligence in England, but there was no way intelligence would tell the RCAF or my family that they had heard about me. It was too dangerous for everybody and they had to be so careful. Most of them had wives and children and, if I had turned out to be an impostor, their house and the neighbour-hood would have been burned down and their families shot. Worse still, the Germans might shoot at least ten of them for each person helped.

It seemed strange to watch the local people passing by the house. They dressed much as we dressed, except a few wore wooden shoes, mostly the farmers or poorer people who couldn't get leather shoes in times like this. My idea of Holland was all windmills, wooden shoes and the girls wearing large skirts. Well, that is what the Dutch people wear for tourist advertisements. The houses were a little smaller but otherwise much the same as ours.

About this time, my wife and mother got their first telegram that I was missing. The telegram was delivered to my mother's sister-in-law, and she came and told my mother. Later that afternoon, I joined the family for a dinner of mashed potatoes. Frits and Klaas and one of the other fellows who was there in the morning, came back and I found out Klaas was a leader of the Underground of that area. He was known as "The Banker" as he lived in a three-story house and had a bank on the main floor. Eep (the teacher) was my main interrogator, as he spoke the best English. He interrogated me for a long time. They wanted to know more about the exact place where I landed. But I had walked in the dark and couldn't tell them very much. I think they would have felt better if they could have found the things that I had buried, but the only real thing I saw was the bush, the big wire fence and the church. They were out looking for my parachute but the Germans had got it first. The Germans knew I was around this general area. They told me it was not safe for me there and I would have to go to another place. My maps and a few things I didn't think I should take, were put in their attic with my name and address. Eep's family thought I had been killed, so a couple years after the war my mother received this small parcel from Holland with these few things in it addressed to the family of R.E. Porter at the address I had left them. My mother had moved over a year previously but the post office finally delivered the parcel to my mother. (I am afraid today it would never get delivered). It was very strange reading the letter they wrote, saying how sorry they were that I had not made it back. After they felt sure I was not an impostor, they decided to move me to another part of town to the home of the Banker. I couldn't go, however, until just before dark. Around 7 o'clock that night we left by bicycle for my new hiding place (this was quite a problem for some who were shot down and could not ride a bicycle.) Eep Bos was going to ride ahead by about the distance between two telephone poles and I was to ride behind acting naturally.

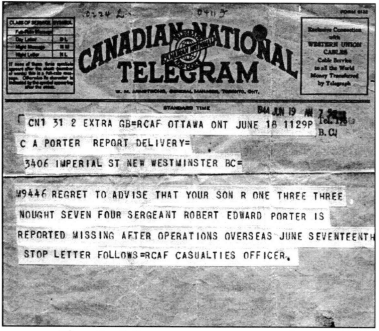

Fig. 3e Telegram sent to my mother

We had a flat tire on the way over and had to stop at a friend of his and repair it. If anyone stopped me, I was to pretend to be deaf and dumb. If that didn't work and I was caught, my story was to be that I didn't know anyone, that I was alone, and no one was helping me. I was supposed to say that I had stolen the bicycle and the clothes. But all went well and we arrived at the two story plus attic building, with a bank on the main floor on Wilhelminastraat (name of the street before the war) just off Hoofdstraat, and now is #5 De Korte Dreef the main road in the village. There were a couple of people around, but Klaas told me to say nothing and walk behind him. Klaas' wife parents were visiting, they lived close by. He took my arm and pushed me right past them. He didn't want the parents to know who I was. After, he told me they remarked, "One would think he was a prisoner or something." Fortunately, they never found out who I was because it would be very dangerous for them to know if I were discovered. We went right upstairs to a small room where Klaas introduced me to his wife Ans. They could speak very little English, but they showed me about the house and made me understand that I would have to stay upstairs. My bedroom on the third floor had a "V" joint ceiling with a trap door and in the centre of the ceiling which could not be seen as it was built right into the V joint. That was my hiding place if anything happened. A radio and earphones were also hidden in the hole and used these to listen to the news.

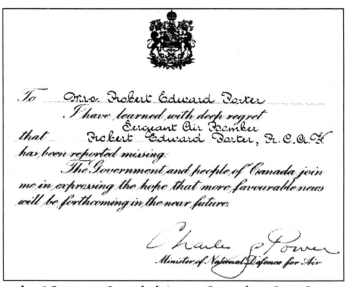

Fig.3f From the Minister of National Defense

"THE LONG RETURN"

ROYAL CANADIAN AIR FORCE
OVERSEAS

IN REPLY PLEASE QUOTE
FILE NO. *419S/4-112*

NO. 419 (R.C.A.F.)Squadron,
"MOOSE SQUADRON"
22nd June, 1944.

Dear Mrs. Porter:

I deeply regret to inform you that your son, Sergeant Robert Edward Porter, is missing from operations on the night of 16/17th June, 1944. This was a very heavy attack on one of the main German industrial targets, and has since proved to have been very successful. Unfortunately, nothing has been heard of your son's aircraft since time of take-off and its loss can only be attributed to enemy action. There is still quite a possibility, however, that all or part of the crew may have escaped or, at worst, be prisoners of war, but news of this could not be expected for some considerable time.

Your son was with us for two months and during that time took part in eight of the recent attacks on Germany and German help territory. He was a very keen and enthusiastic Air Bomber and he set a very splendid example but took a leading part in the sports program of the Squadron during his off hours. I can assure you that the loss of this very popular and useful lad has been a sad blow to us.

If any further news comes hand, you may rest assured you will be notified immediately.

May I convey my sincere sympathy to you in your great loss and hope with you that better news may follow.

Yours sincerely,

WP Pleasance

(W.P. Pleasance DFC) Wing Commander,
Commanding 419 (R.C.A.F.) Squadron.

Mrs. C.A. Porter,
3406 Imperial St.,
New Westminster, B.C., Canada

Fig.3g June 22 (copy of letter) sympathy from my Squadron

75

ADDRESS REPLY TO : THE SECRETARY DEPARTMENT OF NATIONAL DEFENSE FOR AIR, OTTAWA, ONTARIO	OUR FILE *R 133074 (R.O.4.)* REF. YOUR _____ DATED _____

ROYAL CANADIAN AIR FORCE

A I R M A IL   ***OTTAWA***, Canada, 23rd June, 1944.

Mr. C.A. Porter,
3406 Imperial Street,
New Westminster, B.C.

Dear Mr. Porter:

It is with deep regret that I must confirm our recent telegram informing you that your son, Sergeant Robert Porter, is reported missing on Active Service.

Advice has been received from the Royal Canadian Air Force Casualties Officer, Overseas that your son and the entire crew carry out bombing operations over Sterkrade, a suburb of Essen, Germany, on the night of June 16th and the early morning of June 17th, 1944.

The term "missing" is used only to indicate that his where about is not immediately known and does not necessarily mean that your son has been killed or wounded. He may have landed in enemy territory and might be a Prisoner of War. Esquires have been made through the international Red Cross Society and all other appropriate sources and I wish to assure you that any further information received will be communicated to you immediately.

Attached is a list of the members of the Royal Canadian Air Force who were in the crew of the aircraft together with the names and addresses of their next-of-in. Your son's name will not appear on the official casualty list for five weeks. You may, however, release closing the date, place or his unit.

Permit me to extend to you heartfelt sympathy during this period of uncertainty and I join with you and the members of your family in the hope that better news will be forthcoming in the near future.

Yours sincerely,

J.E. Todd s/o

R.C.A.F. Casualty Officer,
for Chief of the Air Staff.

R.C.A.F. G. 32B
500M--1-44(3778)
H>Q>885-G-32B

Fig.3h June 23*rd *(copy of letter) from casualty Officer

Buzzers in the rooms on the second and third floors provided warning signals; the button was downstairs in Klaas' office. One ring was for me to go upstairs and stay in my bedroom when a stranger entered; two rings meant danger! In the later case, I was to run upstairs, get into the hole and hide. These hiding places were very well built and thought out, containing one bottle of water to drink and another for relieving the bladder in case of an extended period of hiding. A few people had been caught by not having the second bottle. It was necessary to have a good warning system to protect Klaas' son Kees. If the family was caught hiding me or helping an Allied airman they would all be shot. However, they were doing this for the freedom of the Netherlands, expecting neither reward nor recognition because no one knew what they were doing. The people in the Dutch Underground were the bravest people I have ever met! The family had quite a few English books and an English-Dutch dictionary. I sat and read (or tried to read.) The days were long as I had never been very good at being alone. They brought my meals up to me, but they ate downstairs, as their family was there and it was not safe for me to go down. At night, they would come up and talk or try to talk, but it is very hard when each of us only spoke a little of the other's language. Although Klaas could speak a little English. Eep would come around and talk. He put signs on the door, wall, lamp, book and every where in the room printed in Dutch and English what each one was. He tried hard to teach me Dutch but I found it very hard to get my tongue around the words. Ans couldn't very much, but we would sit and try to talk. It was a lot of work when you had to look up every word you said. They tried to teach me a little Dutch but I found it very hard to learn as so much of the sound comes from way down in the throat.

Fig.3i Klaas and Ans van Middelkoop's home

Sometimes Eep or Frits would come over some evenings to talk with me and would try to teach me some Dutch. After dark, they would take me out in the back yard for a little exercise and fresh air, but we had to be very careful as there was a curfew at 10 o'clock. Time went very slowly. It was a little hard on the nerves wondering if the Germans would come and search the house. In Holland there were thousands of Jews, airmen like myself, and also young fellows who went into hiding to avoid being sent to labour camps in Germany. The Dutch in hiding were called "Divers" and the Germans spent a lot of time looking for them. You also had to watch out for the

NSBs (National Socialist Party), who were Dutch people sympathetic to the Germans. These collaborators were very cruel, many of them more dangerous than the Germans. All these people in hiding not only had to be hidden but also fed. They had no ration cards, so food had to be found for them. They couldn't go out of the house or dare to be seen by the neighbors. If the Germans had any idea someone was hiding in the house they would make a search, mostly in the middle of the night.

Fig.3j Klaas, Ans, myself and their son Kees

Every once in awhile they would search every house in town but most of them had good hiding places. You would have to be careful if the Germans made a surprised raid at night. If you were in bed you would have to turn your mattress over before you went to your hiding place because they would feel if the bed was warm. The food here was good and I liked the place. Klaas and Ans were very nice people. However, after about 10 days, they said I would have to go and stay at another place. It seemed that the Underground had a secret telephone they used only in emergencies. They had used the phone, called Klaas' number and the Germans had found out. My next hiding place was kept secret, with not even Klaas and Ans being told where I was going; in case they were captured and tortured, they could not tell what they did not know.

Frits came the next day and he took me to a street corner and left me there. They did not know who was going to pick me up, and the person picking me up never knew who brought me. It was very well organised and had to be as safe as possible for everyone. A policeman in uniform soon came along, and turned out to be my contact. He was a big man, very calm, very quiet, but only spoke a couple words of English (a policeman in uniform could be out at night as if he was on duty.) Again, all I was told was to walk naturally. The policeman introduced himself as "Rakers". If you didn't know their real name you couldn't tell anyone who they were. Everyone had a pseudonym or a alias. You very seldom knew their real name and only referred to them by their Underground name or just their first name. We walked down the street for a block or so. There were a couple of men in black uniforms who I found out later were NSB. When we got across from them, Rakers stopped, took out a package of smokes and offered me one. We lit up. He was very calm; I don't think I was. We walked on to where a car was waiting down the block, got in, and drove off. The driver was "The Gardener," at least that's what Rakers referred to him as. I learned later that his name was Copyn and he talked with a bit of a Scottish accent. We drove about a half an hour to the city of Utrecht. With a policeman in the car I felt sort of safe. A couple of blocks from where I was going, we stopped, Rakers and I got out, and we walked to the house where I was to stay. It was one of a large row, like duplexes, except not just two but ten joined together called row houses. We went to one near the centre, whose occupant turned out to be an older lady by the name of Mrs. De Baai. I never found out if that was her real name, but she was English.

She was expecting me. She had two daughters, one a school teacher who spoke English well but the other one spoke very little English. It was a nice home and they were very nice people. They took me upstairs and showed me my room. It had a hole in the ceiling for hiding. It was a good, safe place. The hole was even big enough to put my bed clothes in. I had a bath that night that I will never forget. Mrs De Baai put the water in, brought out some bath salts and hair shampoo and before I could say anything she had put the bath salts in the water. I am sure they would have enjoyed them just as much as I did.

I had to stay upstairs most of the time, as we were on the main street where people could see right into the house from the street. The days were long again. I had lots of English books to read and jig saw puzzles to do, but doing nothing physical all day got tiresome. I had a ration of a package of tobacco a week (Rakers would give it to me) which I had to use carefully. I used to roll my butts and tried to cut my matches half but found that didn't work. It was so hot in the evenings that I would go downstairs and the family would then pull the blinds or we would sit in the dark and talk. The oldest daughter was very interested in England and the rest of the world and what was going on. So much had gone on that they had never heard about, as they only received news the Germans wanted them to hear during approximately four years under the German's occupation. Mrs De Baai's husband was a flyer with Royal Dutch Air Lines (KLM). He had been in Italy when the Germans invaded and they later heard from the Red Cross that he was in the Royal Air Force in England. " I got some relief by listening to the BBC news over a radio hidden in the cellar. Radios were only used for news." If anybody was caught with a radio, they were shot or sent to a concentration camp.

Food was not as plentiful here as at the last place. We were in the centre of the city and food rationing was very tight, especially with an extra person, like myself, who they had to share with. Your bread ration was put on your plate and you knew that was all there was. I didn't understand this at first because bread was something that always seemed to be plentiful in our life, both for the rich and for the poor. The family got their vegetables by going out to the country and buying vegetables. However, bread and meat from the farmers were in very short supply. Once a week they got meat for the four of us. The week's ration was about the same size as a small steak but very tasty. There was also porridge which was a luxury because it was made with buttermilk. I couldn't talk them into using water with a little milk on top. Their coffee was made by boiling milk with a little very black coffee added. "It was really ersatz, a poor imitation of the real drink, since little or no real coffee was available." It was another luxury item, but when I think back to those times, anything to eat was a luxury. Even electricity and gas were rationed affecting all their cooking and heating. There was very little soap and what you did get wasn't like soap, because it would not make a lather. So they washed their clothes in cold water with little or no soap and rubbed them on a board. Before the war, they had sent everything to the laundry, but I guess if we think back to pre-wars days lots of people did not have washing machines.

One day, after I had been there for a week or so, I was sitting out in the back yard in the sun. The neighbor was a gossip and I guess she got to wondering who I was. She saw me there, stuck her head over the fence and started talking to me in Dutch. She caught me by surprise. I couldn't carry a conversation and didn't know what she was saying anyhow. So I just nodded a few times as she talked on then went into the house I told Mrs. De Baai. They became concerned so they got in touch with Rakers. They didn't want to take a chance on leaving me there, but I enjoyed it there and didn't like to leave. At the same time the next day I had to leave. Life was very fragile!

I had time, I was starting to get anxious and wanted to get back to England as the war seemed to be going very slowly. The Allied armies were still fighting in France and the end of the war looked a long way off.

Fig.3k Rakers always in his uniform

I heard from Rakers that there was a scheme to arrange for a number of evaders to meet near the Zuider Zee, where a British aircraft would pick us up. However, the plan never put into effect. This all seemed like a movie to me, where I imagined a group of us would be waiting by the sea with a plane coming in at dusk to pick us up, and these things were happening somewhere I guess. "Many things were happening all around me, of which I did not always have a clear understanding, and I would sometimes pinch myself to make sure I wasn't dreaming."

Rakers did not speak very much English, but I could generally follow what he was saying.

Fig.31 Rakers Different Looks for disguise

He was always so damn cool as he did his thing whether it was his police work or underground work. I was also told of another escape route down through Belgium and across France to Spain. However Rakers did not like this route because he had a feeling about it and never wanted me to go. After the war I found out he had good reason for his caution. Many people were caught going through Belgium, turned over to the Gestapo and put in camps. Many more were simply shot. The next day, in his police uniform, Rakers came with an extra bicycle for me, telling the Baai's family that was best if I moved to a safer house.

We rode off. I kept a safe distance behind him. I had a very strange and frightened feeling not knowing where I was going. I had to be very alert to keep far enough behind him for safety but not too far to lose him. If I did get separated, I would not know where I was or where I was

85

going. He couldn't tell me what to do as he couldn't speak much English. We rode a few miles out of the city via the back roads, until we came to a small village called Groenekan, located on the road to Hilversum. Near the end of the village, we came to a house with a sign on it saying Police. Of course it was written in Dutch, but I guessed it was his place. His wife spoke some English so we could talk and understand each other. "They told me that I had to stay here for a few hours as the American lady wasn't home, and they had not been able to get in touch with her about the change in plan." We had lunch and then supper as they still could not get in touch with the American lady. We slept there that night and the next morning Rakers was told that it had been decided I would stay in his house with his wife and family. I called his wife Mamma as both the children and her husband called her that. I didn't know what else to call her so the name stuck. Dicky (Mamma) was 32 years old and very happy-go-lucky. I do not think she liked the idea of me, a young Canadian flyer and married, going to stay with a American lady living alone. (I thought it was a good idea but I never had the choice.)

Dickie- Hans -Theo 1945

Fig.3m Dicky (Mamma), Hans and Theo

They had two young boys, Hans and Theo, who were four and five years old. I was again impressed by the risk they took in keeping me. "They told the boys that I was their Uncle from a province in north Holland. The dialect spoken there is so different that it could not be understood in this part of the country." So the boys did not suspect I was an Allied evader. This was going to be my home and they made me feel right at home. It was as safe here as any place. Who would expect a respectable Dutch policeman, an ex-army captain working for the Germans, to be hiding a Canadian flyer and later up to six Canadian soldiers in the house. He was a policeman and even more he was the Commandant of the Dutch Underground in that area with responsibility for getting ration cards for Jewish people in hiding, Divers and people like myself. He frequently collected food from farmers and distributed it around. He helped to look after and feed almost two hundred people. He was also able to move people like myself as, being a policeman in uniform, he could travel and be out after curfew. He also had to serve as a policeman and was called out many times by the Germans. He was one of the bravest men I have ever met, and his wife, Dicky, was all ways right behind him.

I later found out June the sixteenth the night I got shot down, was not a good night. There was 321 aircraft on the raid to Sterkrade/Holten: 162 Halifaxes, 147 Lancasters, 12 Mosquitoes. Approx. 21 bombers were shot down by night fighters and a further 10 by Flak.

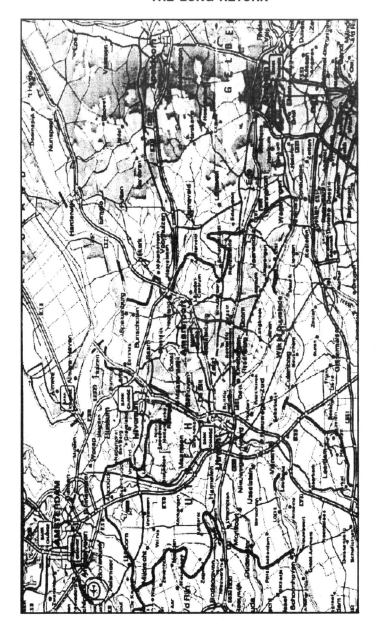

Fig.3n Map of Holland where I was

June Sixteenth to Rakers

```
CITY POLICE    Witness by
OF Zeist,      The Mayor of Zeist,
No: 2158       June 21st, 1944
```

OFFICIAL - REPORT

On June 17th, 1944, at about 0210h, a report was received, that a burning plane crashed onto the Utrechtscheweg in Zeist. Simon Dam, Chief Sergeant of the City Police of Zeist and Special Constable, went as " Chief Crash Investigator" of the Lbd (Luchtbeschermings dienst, A.R.P.) on order of the Opperluitenant(Opper = general, kuitenant = lieutenant) of Police, Evert Herman Neppelenbroek, Local Chief of the Lbd, to the location, and found, a plane burning on the property Utrechtseweg 48, inhabited by Jhr. C.A.de Pester.

The wreckage was located in an open space, about 50 m from the house, and for the most part, was totally burned. The fire was extinguished by the local fire-brigade.

Upon investigation, we found that the crashed airplane was a four-engine English Bomber.

Except for the bomber crew, no human or animal was killed or injured, and no damage was caused.

I went to the location immediately upon being informed of this incident, and ordered the medical picket back as they were not needed.

Later a report came in that bodies were found in two locations in the neighbourhood of the crash site, probably members of the crew. A report was able also received that, in the Torenlaan in Zeist one of the survivors was found.

On order of the German authorities, the bodies were taken to the mortuary of the policy office in Zeist, while the arrested airman was taken immediately to the Ortskommandantur by the already mentioned Oberlt. Neppelenbroek.

Later it became evident that another two airmen were found, in the wreckage of the airplane, but their bodies were not recovered.

The airplane was guarded by a German military sentry.

Two men of the airplane have still not been found.

Reports were received throughout the morning of a part of the plane having fallen in the area. As far as possible, these were taken by motor transport to the German Authorities. Where the parts were to large or to awkward to transport, they were guarded by a policeman.

All this has been done on orders of the Ortskommandant in Zeist. For A.R.P. purposes, 35 litres of petrol was used.

The above was made on oath of office in Zeist and signed on June 18th, 1944.

Seen: The Captain of Police and Commandant of the Lbd.

Fig.3o June 21st 1944. German Police report from Zeist (Translated to English)

Chapter Four

Rakers to Roger Coming

I had more freedom at the Rakers' house, as there were not so many neighbours close by. I slept upstairs and spent the rest of the day downstairs or out in the yard, except when someone came who shouldn't know who I was. At first I just sat around and read, but soon started doing little things around the place and began to feel at home.

Fig.4a Rakers' house

92

I made progress in learning to speak a little Dutch and they learned a lot of English. Dicky Rakers knew a lot of the basics and only needed the practice on speaking English good. However, papa was not around very often, so he really only learned a little.

It was very interesting staying there! I met many men of the Underground, listened to what they were doing, and how they were doing it. It was very exciting and, at times, very scary, especially if you stopped to think what could happen. How soon it could all be over! These men were unbelievable. They were careful and cautious but took very big chances with their lives.

Frits used to come around every once in awhile. One day he came in for morning coffee and said: "I have to go in hiding for a while." The week before, the Underground had scheduled a meeting in town at one o'clock. Something held him up and he was 15 minutes late. As he rode up on his bicycle, something did not seem right, so he rode past very slowly before going in. The Gestapo had found out about the meeting and they were there. They captured eight men that day, but I didn't find out what happened to them. (It would not have been very nice). Frits was very lucky and got away , but now he had to be careful not to seen for a while. However, since he was a very important man, he had to continue his activity in the Underground. About a month later, he was caught in a house where a Jew was hidden and was put in a concentration camp for six weeks. Fortunately, the Germans couldn't find any incriminating evidence about him, so they let him go, but he was a completely different man when he got out. He seemed quite a bit older, very pale and thin. A man can change a lot in six weeks of hell.

We really learned how they could torture a person to the breaking point to try and make one talk. This is why very few people knew each other's real name. There were very few introductions and people kept to their nicknames. To get information, the Gestapo would stick a suspect's head in a tub of water and whack him on the buttocks. They would hit your testicles until they bled. You would be put on a starvation diet, just enough to be kept alive, deprived of sleep and beaten terribly. They would put you in solitary, in a very small room with no light so that, you would not know if it was day or night. If you could go to sleep you would never know if you had slept for five minutes or five hours. Or they would do the opposite: keep you under bright lights and not let you sleep, smash your fingers or break your knees. You cannot think of a torture they would not put you through.

Things were riskier at the Rakers' house as I had no hiding place. It was planned that if necessary I would go out by the window and onto the roof. One day we were visited by a man and woman who were known as the "Hiding Place Makers," because of their main job in the Underground. They proceed to make a hiding place for me in the corner of my bedroom. They cut a hole in the wall which was in the overhang of the eves and this led to a little passage around the house. The door was a bookcase which pivoted by the corner and the back of the book case was filled with bricks so there would not be a hollow sound if the Germans tapped the wall. It was kept full of books and we could lock it from the inside. It was a great hiding place. I almost had to use it a couple of times but the real test never came. The Germans were very smart and had a lot of practice looking for people, so one had to try and be just a little smarter and have a lot of luck. The door was left open all the time so it would not make any marks on the floor when it was closed. If anything happened, I could just throw my clothes in the hole and get in. My water bottle, the other bottle and a few odds and ends were always available. "The Divers, Jewish people in hiding, and Allied evaders all had to be supplied." They all had to be supplied with ration books every month, which was a big job. To accomplish this, the Underground would make the odd raid on the ration offices which were very heavily guarded by the police. Rakers was in charge and made a spare key for the safe. On one occasion, Frits, Rakers and a couple of other fellows planned a raid with the chief of police whose name was Klaasen. The guard that night was a good Dutchman but one of the raiders didn't know this and hit him on the head. He was sure mad at them. Afterwards, he used to come around to the house once in awhile and they used to tease him for not getting out of the way.

The chief of police, Klaasen, organised another raid one night when there were lots of ration cards on hand. It was one of the biggest raids ever made, getting thousands of sheets of coupons. Somehow the Germans found out it was Klaasen who was involved and went to his house to arrest him. When he arrived at home, he saw the German cars in front of his house, so he lay in a nearby ditch.

House of Commons
Canada
Ottawa, July 18th, 1944.

Dear Mr. Porter:-

It is with deep regret I learned of your son on Active Service being listed as 'Missing' from flying operations Overseas.

Whilst I realize that mere words are of little solace at times like these still I felt it only fitting that I should write and tender you my sincere sympathy and also in the hope that word may eventually be received by you as to your boy being still alive.

In the offering of their lives and the sacrifice of the same the Nation owes these gallant boys a debt of gratitude which can never be truly paid.

Mr. C. A. Porter,   Yours sincerely,
1406 Imperial St.,
New Westminster, B. C.   *Tom Reid M.P.*

Fig. 4b July 18th. *Tom Reid, Member of Parliament*

148 WOLVERLEIGH BLVD.
TORONTO
August 17 Th., 1944

Dear Mrs. Porter:

Thank you so much for your letter, I received it yesterday. It was a relief to know you had heard no further word either, I have heard from Mrs. Taylor, of Grafton, Ontario and Mrs. Wilson of Guelph, and I was terribly sorry to hear of their news.

My husband Bill, who was the Navigator on the plane, sent me a number of pictures of Bob's wedding in Wales, no doubt they are the same ones as your Bob sent to you. They seemed to have enjoyed themselves together and they certainly are a fine group of boys. Bill often mentioned Bob in his letters and they seemed very close friends, so I think that wherever they are, they are together. But I feel sure that we shall hear good rews very shortly and let me assure you that I shall write just as soon as any word at all reaches me. I received a very lovely letter from the Padré of the Squadron and he mentioned if he heard anything he would write and let me know. It certainly is a very trying time for us all but I still feel sure that everything will be all right in the end.

Your son, who is training at Brockville would be most welcome anytime he would care to call on me I should enjoy a chat with him - please tell him, won't you?

Bill has a brother in the Navy stationed at Halifax just now but he expects to be coming home on leave for two weeks sometime in September - it will be nice to see him for he hasn't been home in over a year. I have a brother but luckily he is too young for the services, unfortunately if the war keeps up much longer, he too, will have to go. Thank you again for writing Mrs. Porter, it was so nice to hear from you. I too, must ask forgiveness for the typewritten letter but I am sure that you will find it much easier to read than my handwriting would be.

Sincerely,

Dorothy Gardiner

Fig.4c (copy of letter) my mother received from my navigator's Wife

Klaasen had a gun ready, but how can one man fight a dozen well-armed soldiers? When he didn't come home, the Germans took his wife, nine month old twins and three year old son. Klaasen couldn't give himself up as he would have only been shot and maybe others too. His wife and children were put in a concentration camp where the children were separated from their mother. She didn't see them most of that time and the babies were not looked after properly. Klaasen grew terribly old not knowing what was happening to any of them with his picture on display everywhere, he had to go in hiding and keep moving to different places. He sure changed in a few days. He grew a moustache and his hair turned grey by itself. His wife could not tell them anything because she didn't know anything. After a month and a half she and the children were released from the concentration camp but her husband could see her for only a short period every once in a while, as the Germans were still watching her very closely knowing he would visit her. In the Underground Rakers' group there was a very cute young Dutch girl called Vonny. She looked only seventeen or eighteen although I found out later that she was twenty years old. She worked in the ration office from where they distributed all the ration cards in the district. The first time I met Vonny she came in to the house and right into the front room I didn't know who she was. She had a smoke in her hand and said in Dutch, "Have you got a match." I just looked at her dumb and said nothing. Rakers was out in the yard and she went out and she said to him, "Is that fellow in there stupid or what?" Rakers said, "No, he does not speak Dutch, he is a Canadian flyer." She almost died, she could hardly believe it. We became good friends after that. Rakers was generally the policeman in charge when the Germans distributed the ration cards. He had to be very strict and very careful as there were German guards around watching him but he was a little lenient with Vonny. Near quitting time she would take a full sheet of ration cards, sneak them into the washroom, and wrap them around herself under her clothes. Then she would bring them to our place and Rakers would distribute them to people who were in hiding. Sometimes Vonny and people like her would carry them under a girdle. Vonny could not speak much English but who needs to talk? She used to say, "You and me together in Canada." Dicky would say, "None of that around here. He is a married man!" Vonny was always a bright spot in my life. I always looked forward to her coming around. If we happened to end up in a room alone, Dicky would bang on the door and say, "What are you two doing in there?" I used to say Dicky, "You're a poor sport" and she would always answer back, "You are a married man." I guess I always had "a girl weakness." One day when I was working in the garden, Vonny arrived and sprayed water on me. I was not thinking and chased her down the street, shouting after her in English. My God, the chances we would take! Rakers came home when we were down the street and he was furious with us.

One of the key jobs of the Underground was to provide forged identity documents for Divers or any person in trouble with the Germans. I had my own identity card which was called a "Persoonsbewijs." My name was "Henk De Graaf." and it stated that I was deaf and dumb.

Fig. 4d Vanny

I also had papers saying I was a farmer who didn't have to go work in Germany. I had taken the identity of a boy who had died many years ago.

When I had my picture taken I went in to the photographer's shop with Rakers. I never said a word. We had gone into Utrecht which was six or seven miles on the bicycle. As usual, I was told to say nothing. Rakers and the photographer did all the talking and I thought I had done very well. However, as we were leaving the shop, the photographer winked and said, "Good night" in perfect English, I smiled and kept on going. It never got into a situation outside the house where I had to act deaf and mute in front of any Germans or German Sympathizers but there were many times inside that an awkward situation arose with Dutch visitors. Someone would come who wasn't safe or who we didn't know if they could be trusted. I would have to stay mute and generally I had a Dutch book which I pretended to read. I was always careful not to have it upside down. We had heard about an airman in France, travelling on a train, pretending to read but he was holding his book upside down. He got caught. That was a very good lesson to remember.

Fig.4e   **Fig.4f**
They would put the Machine gun in the baby buggy
and then put the baby on top

One day, a Dutch policeman named Jan Bakker came to the village. He had been transferred from down south. As he couldn't find a place to stay, Rakers had to take him in. Rakers wasn't sure if he was safe or not, and wasn't sure if he was going to stay in our village permanently. If he wasn't going to stay it was best that he didn't know who I was so I had to be deaf and dumb for five days. It was sure a hard job, requiring a lot of concentration. At meal times I would go to ask for something and then, remembering, would have to nod to someone for it or someone would go to speak to me. On some occasions, we would be left alone in the room and I would be afraid to look him in the eye in case he said something. However, I guess he just thought I was a bit stupid, not just deaf and dumb. After five days they decided he was going to stay and they had an opportunity to check up on him. As soon as he passed the security check, they told me I could tell him who I was. When I started to talk to him in English, I thought his eyes would pop out of his head. I told him that he was a hell of a policeman as he could not spot a Canadian airman. "He was completely surprised, not having had the least suspicion of who I was."

In about a month, I knew enough Dutch to be able to say a few things like "Good morning," "Good night" and could understand enough to know what people were talking about. I knew when to nod or smile and I was safer to have around. The baker and the green-grocer would see me and I could say good morning to them. If they started to talk too much, and I couldn't answer them with yes or no, I would get up and walk off. They thought I was indifferent, angry, or just moody and never guessed who I was.

The Rakers lived in a side by side duplex and the man who lived next door was a National Socialist person and a postman. They never guessed who I was. I would say, "Good morning," or "yes" or "no" or some simple things, without arousing any suspicion. One day, I was standing on the back porch and the postman was talking to me over the fence. Dicky was standing behind me to be sure I didn't get into trouble. We talked for five or ten minutes with me just nodding or saying, "yes" or "no." Dicky was making sure I was not getting into trouble with him. After the war, Dicky was talking to him and he said, "Did your nephew get back home OK." She said, "Yes, he is back in Canada". He just stared in amazement. By now my mother had received a couple of letters from people giving her sympathy, as she still did not know what had happened to me.

In August, after I had been at Rakers about two months, Rakers felt I could do with a change. I went into Utrecht for a couple weeks to stay with some other people who spoke English well. This was my holiday. The Heitinga family had spent a lot of time in England before the war. They had two very nice daughters Shelah, a student seventeen years old, and the other, a little older, Eileen who was a dancer on the stage. (They were lovely). They lived in a town house that was part of a big three story square block of houses with a balcony all around. I slept on the third floor and my escape place was a trap door in the floor, leading into the false top of a linen closet on the floor below. The family was very nice and it was wonderful to be able to speak English all the time.

Mr. Heitinga, an architect in Holland and Belgium, doing displays for large exhibits and theatres, all over Europe, had had a lot of money before the war. When the Germans invaded, they confiscated his big house. They had come on a Friday night and said the family had to be out by the Monday.

The Germans took a list of all the furniture and drapes, and warned them not to try to take any furnishings with them. The Heitinga's then found this town house whose Jewish occupant had just been sent to Germany. The neighbours were not very friendly with the Heitingas, believing they had something to do with the Jewish people getting sent to Germany.

Fig.4g Shelah Heitinga

Fig.4h Eileen Heitinga

Food was very scarce in the city. Often, we would be lucky to have an apple for breakfast but they said that there was very little sugar diabetes and things like that in the wartime. Maybe the diet was not that bad. After the war the Heitingas had a very big problem but I will go into that in more detail later in the story. I had a lot of English books to read and a radio in my hiding place for the news. But I never was a very good reader. I was by myself a lot of the time, as the family had other things to do. Their lives were very busy. Of course I could not go out or be seen by anybody. Rakers had given me a little tobacco and as I was a smoker this was very nice! About this time, the British and American forces were advancing through France and up into Belgium.

We listened to the news four or five times a day, expecting our liberation in a few weeks. That was August 1944, but the liberation was not to be for another nine months. Of course when you are watching the news day by day, it goes by slowly, just like waiting for a kettle to boil.

The Allies got as far as Belgium and just seemed

Fig.4i Mr. Heitinga

to stay there. After a week or so I went back to Rakers' place, because it was much safer and more exciting to hear of what was going on and also would go for the odd bicycle ride. I would recognise many of the different Underground people as Rakers' house which was the centre of a lot of activities. Sometimes I would work in the garden. They had some different weeds and the vegetables seemed different in Netherlands, so I was pulling the vegetables and leaving the weeds. Once I found an old fellow standing, looking over the fence and staring, who asked me what I was doing in the garden but Rakers was there to answer for me, otherwise I would have just had to ignore him.

Fig 4j Mrs Heitinga

Rakers took many risks. For example, the Underground had planned a special raid in Amsterdam and needed some guns. Since Rakers was able to travel with no problem and as a policeman, wore high boots, leggings and a large leather coat, he went into Amsterdam carrying twenty six revolvers strapped on his legs, body and in his pockets. They almost completely weighed him down. He sat next to a German officer on the train but, as always very cool, and everything went well.

He left on these trips as if he was going to the corner store, yet he often went off in the morning and never knew when he would be back. He would come back and have supper then go out again, coming home at ten or eleven o'clock. Being a policeman, he could be out at night. Not many others had such freedom, so he had to do a lot of the night work. He told Dicky very little, so if either of them were caught, neither one could tell anything.

In September our electricity was completely cut off. The Netherlands produced its electrical power from coal and all their coal was going to the war. The Dutch cook mostly on electric stoves. To solve this problem, Rakers climbed the pole and put a thin wire jumper between the main lines and ours. It didn't provide enough electricity to run the stove but we could have a couple of lights on or the radio on for news. We would pull the drapes tightly over the windows so no one could see that the lights were on. The Germans allowed everyone one sack of coal every once in a while but that did not last long. Rakers found an old wood cook stove which we patched up and made to work. Any old stove was worth a fortune. However, wood was almost impossible to get so we gathered bits of wood from everywhere.

Rakers once bought a tree about a foot and a half thick and not very tall in a farmer's wood lot. He must have made some sort of deal with the farmer as it was marked. When we got to the farm to pick it up, we had to cut it, then haul it home. While we were cutting the tree in the woods, a German officer, who was hunting, came up to us. Rakers knew him as a result of his police duties. Rakers always wore his uniform as we stood there and they talked, I could understand enough of what they were saying to know when to nod or smile. He never guessed my identity and finally walked off. It was funny how close one can come and not be caught. But I noticed that Rakers had kept his hand close to his gun. Everybody played for keeps and I am sure Rakers would have shot him if it had been necessary.

After we cut the tree up and were on our way home with our wood in the farmer's horse-drawn wagon, the farmer said something to me. Hans, Papa Rakers' four year old boy was there and said, "That's my Uncle from Groningen. His Dutch is different from our Dutch." I smiled and said nothing. That explanation was a lot better than expecting the children to be so very careful not to tell anyone that I was Canadian.

The British were bombing very heavily these days. Main highway, the Hilversum road, ran along the front of the house and a railway ran along the back of the house. Very often the allied fighter bombers would dive bomb over the house, bombing either a train on the railway or trucks on the highway. I found this difficult, sitting right there, not knowing if they were trying to hit the railway or the highway or would just hit us in between. They flew so low that I felt I could almost touch them. I always thought about the pilots having their ham and eggs in a hour or so. I felt I was so far away from England and yet so close, but yet so far away. Eggs in Holland were almost impossible to get. If you could get them, they were very expensive on the black market and I don't think I ever saw any ham. They had a little bacon once in a while but it was cured a little more than ours and not smoked as much.

One day, some of the fellows of the Underground brought some small boxes of explosives around to the house. They had been dropped by the British for blowing up the railways. However, the explosives had to be put together, sealed and the timer put in with directions in both Dutch and English, we all sat at the dinner table figuring out how to wire them and just how best to set them off. The plan was to blow up each railway line coming out of Utrecht. Each Underground unit was to be ready when the orders came to blow them all up at a certain time. At this exact time there would also be aircraft flying over, on their way to a target in Germany, so the Germans would be confused about where and how the bombing was being done. The important thing was to keep the Germans confused for a while, to give the Underground time to get home or into hiding.

Once assembled, the bombs were taken out and attached to the railway tracks. Rakers placed his bombs on tracks close to home, so he had time to come back before they went off. We stood in the dark in the back yard and waited for the explosions. Each set of bombs had been set for intervals of a few minutes or so and, because they were well scattered, the Germans didn't know which way to go. It was like Halloween!

One of the railway lines that Rakers blew up was just at the end of the row of houses in which I was living. Some of the residents heard the aircraft overhead, the bombs going off, and ran out of their houses through a big ditch filled with water to cross the road away from the tracks. They would wait there awhile, then go back just as another bomb went off. They would then runback through the ditch full of water and again wait for a while, until they were sure the bombing was over. They did not know where the bombing was coming from but naturally they figured it was from the bombers flying overhead. They were sure angry, getting wet and muddy every time they had to cross the big ditch into the field. Of course they were also very frightened. They never found out that it was Rakers who was setting the bombs off. It was a very successful night and almost everyone was pleased, except the Germans of course. It was funny when people came around in the morning and told us about it. De Burgomaster, (The Mayor), phoned Rakers up and told him all about the damage caused by the sabotage.

All went well except for one real tragedy. A group of fellows, who were blowing up one of the other rail lines, had a bad break. A German soldier shot one of them, although the others got away. The next day the Germans went to his home, asked for his father and shot him at the door. The Germans then went into the house and destroyed everything. They opened up food, ate some, threw the rest all over the house and then they destroyed all the furniture. That's the price the Dutch had to pay. The families of the ones that got caught had to pay very harshly. The Germans had a very hard time in Holland as the average Dutch person just did not co-operate with them. The Germans wanted to burn all the houses along the railway track that had been damaged, but the Mayor talked them out of it. There was a small town in Holland where a German officer was shot and killed. The Germans moved in and gave all the people an hour to move out. The Germans then completely destroyed the town, flattening it completely. They brought bulldozers in and buried all that was left of the town, as if it never existed. Many times these things were actually carried out by the (Nationaal Socialistische Beweging.) That was why they were hated so much, even more then the Germans.

They tried to break the spirit of the Dutch people but they never did. It just made the Dutch people stronger and more determined.

By now my mother had received a couple of letters from people giving her sympathy, as she still did not know what had happened to me. Just a telegram saying I was missing on a flight over Germany and a letter from the squadron I was flying from.

ADDRESS REPLY TO:
THE ~~SECRETARY~~.
DEPARTMENT OF NATIONAL DEFENCE FOR AIR,
OTTAWA, ONTARIO.

OUR FILE R133074 (RO-4)
REF. YOUR
DATED

ҡOYAL CANADIAN AIR FORCE

OTTAWA, Canada, 15th September, 1944

Mr. C. A. Porter,
3406 Imperial Street,
New Westminster, B.C.

Dear Mr. Porter:

     I must regretfully inform you that since your son, Sergeant Robert Edward Porter, was reported missing no further information regarding him has been received other than that contained in the letter to you dated June 23rd from these Headquarters.

     You may rest assured that every possible effort is being made to trace your son and upon any news being obtained you will be informed immediately.

     May I extend my sincere sympathy to you and the members of your family in this time of anxiety.

Yours sincerely,

J. E. Thompson S/O

R.C.A.F. Casualty Officer,
for Chief of the Air Staff.

Fig.4k September 15ᵗʰ my Mother received this letter

AIR MINISTRY

73-77 Oxford St., London, W.1.,

31st October, 1944.

CAN/R113074/P.4 CAS

Dear Mrs. Porter,

I greatly regret to inform you that since my lettter of the 20th June, 1944, no further information has been received concerning your husband, Sergeant Robert Edward Porter.

In view of the absence of any news for so long a period it is felt that you should be informed of our grave anxiety for his safety, but action to presume that he lost his life will not be taken until evidence of his death is received, or until such time has elapsed that it is considered there can be no longer any likelihood of his survival. Such action will then be for official purposes only and I will write to you again at that time.

You may rest assured that every possible effort is being made to trace your husband, and upon any news being obtained you will be informed immediately.

May I again express to you my sincere sympathy in this time of great anxiety.

Yours sincerely,

G.E.J. Welsh

(G.E.J. Welsh), Squadron Leader,
for Air Officer Commanding-in-Chief,
Royal Canadian Air Force, Overseas.

Mrs. R.E. Weller,
18 Llwyn Hflyg,
Nantybwgh,
Tredegar,
Monmouthshire. Wales.

Fig.41 Letter of October 31st. Not good news for my wife to receive.

Chapter Five

Roger to January Second

On October 26, 1944 (I will always remember that date), I was awakened at 6 o'clock in the morning by Mr. Ponsen, the caretaker of an old fortress just out of town and also a member of the Underground who won a medal from the Queen. He said he had found a couple of men who claimed that they were Canadian soldiers and did not know what to do with them. They said they had been captured near the Dutch-Belgian border and that they were from the Canadian Scottish Regiment. Both had been taken prisoner and claimed they had escaped from a train coming out of Utrecht. The caretaker wanted me to interrogate the soldiers to make sure that they were Canadian and not Gestapo dressed in Canadian uniforms, trying to infiltrate the Dutch Underground. They were currently hidden in the cold and damp basement of the old unused Fort.

I found the soldiers, dirty, tired, and very hungry. One was a young Captain (who later became a colonel), the other, a private. While I interrogated them,

Rakers stood nearby with his hand on the gun in his pocket, ready to shoot them if the answers were not satisfactory. Roger was both very sick and tired. The Captain seemed so young. His regimental number was different from mine, but of course his number was army and mine Air Force. I asked them many questions about Canada, the army and the English. I had to be very sure. After a couple of hours I was convinced that they were telling the truth.

The Captain, Roger Schjelderup was too sick to ride a bicycle so he had to be left there until dark. He was brought to Rakers' home in the car of a doctor who was also in the Underground. As the Canadians were cold and dirty, they really appreciated a bath, dry clothes and the food they were given to eat. Louis Trainor, the second soldier, was taken to a home in Bilthoven, a few miles up the road, since Rakers' house was full. A few days after Roger was picked up, two of the other soldiers were found by the Underground a few miles north, and homes were found for them in Hilversum. They were Sergeant Amando Gri, nick named "Doc" of Trail, B.C. and Private Harvey Swartz of Vancouver. The next two, Sergeant Major Wilf Berry and Private Marcel Briere, met a group of teenagers who were hiding from the Germans to avoid being sent to Germany to be used as forced labour. The teenagers introduced Wilf and Marcel to a couple in the Underground and they were put up in Bilthoven, a few miles north. Wilf and Marcel were moved two or three times as houses with good hiding places were not easy to find and few people had enough food (Rakers had to keep track of a lot of people, so he would always know of someplace to hide someone.) I went to see them a few times. I was lucky that I had my identity papers and Rakers had a spare bicycle, but it was taking a big chance every time we went out.

The Canadian soldiers had all been captured on a canal Northeast of Brussels. After being captured, they were marched back from the front line and transported to Utrecht where they were interrogated for a week. Later they were put in a box car, taken to a siding and left there for a few days. I guess the Germans were not sure what to do with them and transportation of any kind was very scarce. When the Germans searched them, they didn't find a small jack knife that one of them had hidden. The prisoners started cutting a hole in the floor of the box car which was made of four inches of heavy plank. They got it cut almost right through, but were too well guarded to do much, so they waited for their chance. Eventually the train started to move, heading for a camp in Germany. When they were a few of miles out of town, the train slowed down then stopped. The Canadian soldiers pushed out the hole and eleven of them jumped out. The others in the box car did not want take a chance. Some were more nervous and did not know what to expect. During their train trip before reaching Utrecht, they had stopped at a small station and were being held in a waiting room. Smiley, one of their friends, hid behind the counter when the other POWs were returned to the box car, but the Germans counted heads and found one missing. They went back and found him and, with their rifle butts and their boots, beat him out and all the way down the platform. They then locked him up in the box car at the end. We only found six of the escaped prisoners. The others could have been hiding somewhere else, but six out of the eleven was pretty good odds.

Roger stayed with me at Rakers' house, so we could look after him. The doctor checked him over and found out that he had pleurisy, an inflammation of the lungs. Because he had a big fever, he had to have his bedclothes changed a couple

Fig 5a Doc Van Veelen

of times a day and bathed. Dicky and I looked after him for a few days but it got too much; so Doctor Van Veelen arranged for help from a nurse whose name was "Nellie." She stayed right at the house to look after him. Dicky and I had many laughs, she was very "aloof" when she drank from a cup she would hold her little finger out. Dicky would imitate her and we would break out laughing. She never caught on to what we were doing. Sometimes things got a little boring so we had to have something to amuse us.

Roger was very sick and we were not sure if he would live. We talked about what we would do with the body if he died. Would we dig a hole in the back yard and bury him or maybe take him to a farm yard? Or would we leave him some place with his identity on him so the Germans would find him and the Red Cross would bury him? One thing was for sure, the body could not be found in the police station or in the house. There were too many other lives at stake. But luckily he got better and all was well.

One night Rakers went to a meeting in the village. He didn't think much of it and said he would not be late returning. Ten o'clock was considered late and still no Rakers. Eleven o'clock, then twelve o'clock passed and still he wasn't home. By this time, Dicky and I were getting very nervous. We then began wondering if the Germans had raided the meeting, so I started to gather up all the different Underground papers. It was surprising what was left around. Papers were under the carpet, behind shelves and all over the place. A lot of them were on the dining room table. I put them all in my hiding hole. I then dressed Roger, as sick as he was told him that we may have to get in the hole tonight, and made him practice coughing without making a noise. He was really too sick to give a damn but it could have been a life or death situation. Dicky and I then sat upstairs in the dark looking out of the bedroom window with the hiding hole open and ready to get into. (I don't think I have ever put in such a long three hours). Of course we were thinking the worst.

About one o'clock, we heard gun-fire at the corner. We were sure that the Germans were shooting at Rakers and members of the Under- ground. About one thirty, a big car drove down the road, slowed down next door and almost stopped, then started up again and slowed down in front of our house, then stopped. You could have heard a pin drop. Both of us figured that this was it, and I don't even think we were breathing. We both figured Rakers had been arrested, although neither of us said it, and we were both sure the Germans were coming to raid the house. But then the car drove off. What a relief!

A little while later Rakers came home. He was very calm as if nothing had happened and nothing did happen to him. The meeting had just lasted longer then expected, so all the worry was for nothing. In fact Rakers was a little displeased at us for making such a fuss.

I got nervous at times; we were not exactly playing games, and I was not as calm as Rakers. Rakers and Dicky would have been shot if the Germans had found me in their home. In contrast, I would only be taken to a concentration camp or a prisoner of war camp. With these dangers, you had to try to think of it all as one big game or it would get to you. When lying in bed at night, hearing a car drive up or someone talking outside, I would jump up, look out the window and ask myself if it was a raid or if someone was coming? One tried not to be on edge. For their part, Rakers always seemed very calm and Dicky seemed to take it in her stride. I just cannot get over how brave they really were! When you think of what they were doing for a free Holland, not just taking a chance on their own lives, but those of their family and children, not just eight hours a day, but twenty-four hours a day. In the seven months I was there I don't remember Rakers ever taking a day off. He was always on guard with three identity cards ready in case he had to go on the run.

Food was getting very hard to find by this time. Everything was rationed and even when it was rationed you could not get it very often. There just wasn't any food around and the Germans gathered any they found for themselves or sent it back to Germany. Tobacco did not exist as we know it today. W e would buy green leaves from a farmer, dry them in the attic and cut them into thin strips with a paper cutter. The tobacco it made was very strong and very rank, but when you haven't anything else it's just amazing what one would do for a cigarette. There were a lot of good farmers who would sell food at a reasonable price, but some of them didn't want money. They wanted linen, blankets, gold and silver and people would give their wedding rings for a sack of potatoes.

We were very lucky as to electricity. They cut the power off at the main station but the air raid warning was on a separate power line, just in front of the house. Rakers climbed the pole, tapped into the line with a thin wire and ran it to the line going into the house, giving us enough power for a couple of lights. We had to be very careful to black out all the windows so there was no chance of anyone seeing us with these lights on. If the Germans caught you doing that they would get very upset and, for punishment, take all your furniture, except one table, one bed, one chair, and one set of clothes. The rest would be sent to Germany with a big sign on it saying, "A gift from Holland."

Another winter was coming and the German people were getting cold, even the soldiers. Under the occupation, everybody had to give four blankets, one complete outfit of men's and lady's clothes. As the Dutch had not been able to buy anything for years, they couldn't spare these items but they had to give them anyway. When you gave the clothes, the Germans would put a sticker on your door. If you didn't have a sticker on your door they would come later to take the clothes plus a lot more. The Germans had been fighting a very long war, over five years now, and all of Europe was running out of everything. Nobody dreamed that the war would last this long.

The Germans had taken big losses in Africa, Italy and on the Russian Front. Although they were fighting very hard for survival, it was amazing how high their morale was. They all still believed Hitler would come up with some kind of secret weapon. The latest one was the Buzz Bomb (know as the "Doodlebug" was the VI Vergeltungs waffe No1, Revenge Weapon No1, later we had the V2 rockets). It was very hard on people's nerves because one never knew where it was going to land. The Germans would just send it over the channel to England. You would hear the buzz noise and not worry much, but when the noise stopped you knew it was coming down.

The Allies parachuted into Arnhem and Nijmegen on Sept. 17th, 1944 as part of their drive north. Things got really bad in Arnhem and in Holland in general. The people had already been heavily bombed and now they were caught in the fighting right in town. Something went wrong with the Allies' plans. The British army could not link up with the airborne force and thousands of paratroopers lost their lives or were taken prisoner. At the end of the battle, lots of them were on the loose, hiding in Holland, but I never saw any of them as I was too far north. It was a very bad defeat for the Allies.

After the paratroopers scattered, the "German Hitler Youth" movement (German Hitler Jugend) was sent in. They were fanatic young Nazis who had been trained from a very young age. The Germans took these kids, when they were 12 to 15 years old and sent them to a Nazi school. They were taught to be very proud Aryans and that they were "the master race." They gave them guns and very tough army training. They were like miniature SS troops and many were even worse. They counter-attacked and took back the town with the 9th & 10th SS Panzer Divisions. Of course they were very angry with the Dutch people for welcoming the Allies and giving them full support. The Dutch in Arnhem had thought the war was over and that the Allies were there to stay.

This gave the Germans a great morale booster all over Holland; they were really strutting around again. The Germans started confiscating everything: furniture, clothes, and anything else they could move. They raided all the houses; what they could not take, they destroyed, they put big swastikas on beautiful furniture and walls. If they could not take it, no one else was going to have it. I guess they figured the Allies were not far away. A lot of the people left when the fighting started and were not allowed to go back until after it was over. Most the people in town lost everything. It was getting harder to survive in hiding and even harder to get food. Food was getting very scarce and the German solders were getting more and more on edge. Most of them felt the end was very near, but the real tough SS Nazis never showed any sign of weakening. If a soldier on the streets of Utrecht spoke about losing the war, a German officer would shoot him on the spot.

Rakers' cousin from Amsterdam, Manse, his wife Jo and their little boy came to live with us. This made seven adults and four children in a small three bedroom house. Food in the big city was getting very hard to get. We all helped Dicky with the house work, cooking and cleaning, and Rakers got the food. Where from? I never found out.

A couple of weeks later, Sergeant Major Wilf Berry and Marcel Briere arrived to hide with us. They had been living in a small town north of us, but the people they were staying with didn't have enough food or a proper place for them to hide, and were getting very nervous. Not everyone can live under these circumstances. Rakers' home had three very small bedrooms upstairs, a small front room, a dining room and a kitchen downstairs. In this small space, eight adults and four children were now living, including four of us Canadians. That takes a lot of calmness with the Germans all around. Dicky took it as it came. You can see why 50 years later, I have such tremendous respect for her. Dicky, or Mamma as I called her, will always be a beautiful Lady to me.

In the third week of November I went to stay with Heitinga, in Utrecht; again, a bit of a winter holiday.

As they say, a change is as good as a rest. Things were different with Heitinga. I never really knew what job he did in the Underground. He would keep company with a chauffeur in the German Army, using him to obtain information. In the Underground most people didn't know what any others were doing in case they were caught. However, the Underground had a newspaper and announced that Heitinga was not to be trusted, as he had been seen associating with the Germans. Therefore, he had to be careful with Underground people who didn't know him, as they might have tried to shoot him and, as he worked in the Underground, he also had to be careful of the Germans. He had to keep his doors double locked all the time and just answer to certain knocks. I guess I should have been more nervous there, but I wasn't. Most of the farmers wouldn't sell him any food, so it became very difficult to get food for him and his family. But I fully believe he was good and I trusted him. The Heitingas shared everything they had. Sometimes for breakfast we would just have an apple. People in town were really going hungry and cold now, with little kids begging crusts of bread. If the Dutch couldn't afford the black market or get food from a farmer, they just went hungry. I used to sit, read novels and think, "My God, I am part of a big story and just don't realise it."

I was with the Heitingas for a few weeks when Rakers came to get me. He did not say he was coming; he just showed up. Rakers knew a German who had lived in Holland for many years, before the war. When the Germans invaded Holland, he had to go in the German Army. However, he used to keep in touch with Rakers and tell him what was going on. He now had heard that the Germans were going to search all the houses in town for Divers, so I went back to what I called "home", in Groenekan.

I was never given any notice of when I was to be moved as people never wanted others to know what they were doing. He would just come out of the blue and we'd leave. I never had any possessions so I never had to pack, except for picking up my shaving kit, a pair of socks and a change of underwear. I played a lot of cribbage at Heitingas with their daughters Shelah and Eileen, I taught everyone the game and we had a lot of good times.

December fifth is the Dutch St.Nicholas day, a European custom where they give out presents. All of us dressed up in a suit and tie for this celebration. St. Nicholas and two Zwarte Piet or "Black Peters" are associated with this activity." The Black Peters visit homes carrying a potato bag and if little kids are bad during the year they are always told that Black Peter will put them in the bag instead of giving them presents. For weeks ahead, the kids were scared of Zwarte Piet and were really good. We had St. Nicholas and Zwarte Piet come to the house all dressed up for the kids and me. The one Zwarte Piet was the Westerbeek girl from Hilversum where Wilf was living. She worked in the bank with Vonny. St. Nicholas sat like a judge with Black Peter on each side and read from his book which listed all the good and bad things that the kids had done all year. To please the kids I was put in the sack and played the part of being a bad boy. I didn't know if I was a father or not back in England. A lot was going on around the house at this time. People were coming and going and they were having many meetings as quite a few people had been caught by the Germans. There were also people picking up food. With all this activity, the people next door thought Rakers was in the black market business and that I was a Dutchman from Groningen in northern Holland, and hiding from the Germans. I would have liked to have seen their faces when it was all over and they found out that I was a Canadian, and that Rakers was one of the heads of the Underground. Sometimes there would be a dozen bicycles in the yard. The Germans must have thought he was a very busy policeman, doing his job. Food was getting harder and harder to get. It had been hard all along but much worse now. Some of the farmers would not sell their produce.

The prices got higher, but people just didn't have the money. One night, the Underground raided one of these farmers. They took bicycles, big trailers and large wagons that they pulled. They took all the extra food that the farmer had and he had a lot. It was to be given to the people in hiding who didn't have ration cards, or to people that had neither food nor money to pay the black market. Rakers had organised the raid but he didn't go inside because he knew the farmer and his family. He remained on guard outside. He had to hurry home as soon as it was over because he knew the Mayor or the Germans would be phoning him. It wasn't long before the Mayor of the town did phone and informed him of the raid. Rakers had to go out and investigate the theft. So, he went back to the farm that he had just robbed to try and find out who robbed it. He took down all the particulars and examined the bicycle tracks. He lead the investigation in the opposite direction to keep all suspicions away from his group. A few days later he was sitting in the police station working, not the police house where I lived, when the German police came and said they wanted to see him. He was ready to go out the window and make a run for it because he thought they were after him for Underground work. But they were just checking up on the farms that had been raided. It gave Rakers a scare for a minute but he was real cool, at least on the outside.

Fig.5b St.Nicholas and Black Peter on December. 5th 1944

I guess I will never know how people like this really felt inside. He told the Germans about the raid, told them which way the thieves had left but said that he had lost their track. It was the middle of December 1944 by now. We were all starting to think of Christmas, saving up little things and planning everything. Rakers had bought a rabbit which we kept it in the back shed. We had saved things like a couple of packages of jelly powder; anything to make Christmas a little special. We all helped to clean the house. We all had to do a little work because at this time there were thirteen of us living in a small three bedroom house. There were a lot of things to do.

On the nineteenth of December, we were decorating the house and planning a good time when Frits came on his bicycle. We just thought it was nice of him to come and visit us near Christmas. But then he told us that a group was being organised to cross through the German lines and we would have to leave in two days. He knew very little about it, just that. We were to go to a certain place and be left there. We would then be met by another guide and taken to a small town on the River Waal. We were all very excited about going after waiting all this time. Leaving just a couple of days before Christmas was sort of sad, but also exciting, so many mixed feelings. Dicky was very sad thinking of us all leaving, especially now just before Christmas. Rakers was against it, so was Eep Bos. They figured that there were too many of us travelling together and that we had waited all this time so it would not hurt to wait a little longer, since the Allies were getting closer. No one knew exactly where the orders came from for us to go, but things were getting very tough in Holland and I guess they knew it was going to get even tougher, we had great ideas of what we were going to do. Frits guessed we were going to cross the German lines over Christmas when the Germans were celebrating. Meanwhile, Rakers was very busy as he had a lot of work to do these days. The Germans were getting tougher, sending all young people, or any able bodied person, to Germany. I guess that was the main reason why we were leaving, as it was getting harder and harder to survive, Rakers took me on a quick trip into Utrecht. There I went to see the people where I first stayed, the De Baai family, to say Good-bye to them. I told the daughter, whose father was in England someplace, that I would thank him very much for all they had done for me. As I said he had been a flier before the war and was in Italy when it all started. He had made his way to England, and was a flier in the RAF. We had full hope of being in London in a few days and as I left I thanked them for all they had done for me. Then, we went to see the Heitingas to say Goodbye. I told them, "I will have a drink for you in London, on New Year's Eve". We felt pretty definite that we would be back in England in a couple of days. There was a lot of excitement, saying good-bye to all the people I knew. It was like leaving home and I felt I may never see them again. We had all been so very close. Slim, from the hospital, gave us a quart of straight alcohol, which we mixed with citron and water. It wasn't bad. We had a few drinks each but it didn't go far among ten of us. The next morning,

Amando Gri (Doc) and Harvey Swartz the other two soldiers, came down early in the morning. They had been living with Klaas Scheep-vaart near Maartensdjk. Then a couple of guides came, each guide had brought an extra bicycle and a few other people had left theirs. We took a lunch because we were going to bicycle thirty kilometres. After laying around for months and not doing much, that was a long ride. There were a lot of sad farewells. Dicky, Rakers and I had become very close over the last seven months Dicky had such great plans for Christmas. (They never did eat the rabbit we had kept in the shed for Christmas). Rakers still didn't like the idea of us going.

Fig.5c The day before we left Rakers

Fig.5d The Morning we left Rakers to travel south to Amerogen

He was very nervous about it, feeling it was not safe. Rakers still didn't like the idea of us going. He was very nervous about it, feeling it was not safe. W e rode in pairs, a couple of telephone poles between each pair. I bicycled out of town with Slim whom I had got to know quite well by this time. We had just gone a few miles when one of the bicycles broke down, so one of the guides took the broken one back. We still had a couple of guides. After going ten miles or so, I met the "Teacher" on the road. I broke from the group and went over to talked to him. I was wearing his sweater and other pieces of his clothing back to England. He said "That's OK." He had fixed up my battle dress, had it dyed, and had been wearing it since we changed clothes when I first met up with the Underground. He was very surprised to see me biking down the road and he also did not like so many of us going together. We said farewell, because I had to go very fast to catch up to the others who had cycled ahead.

We went maybe another thirteen miles and were met by our next guide, called Dirk. The other guides left us and Dirk was taking us the rest of the way. He was the one that had organised our escape and was in charge of the operation. He couldn't speak much English, he told our guides what we were to do and they explained it to us. They then said good-bye and left. They had told us, "You have to cross a river in a small barge that is pulled across the River Rhine on a cable. It is powered by the current. There will be a German guard on the ferry. Say nothing, get on it, pushing your bicycle." They then said, "Follow Dirk into the town of Amerogen and go half way through the town. Dirk will stop at a house and you are to go in with him." When we got to the Dutch Rhine we had to go on the little ferry. The guides rode ahead of us. The ferry was like a little barge that ran on a cable and the river current powered it. The guides had given us our money for the ferry and we rode down the bank after them. We got on the barge and we handed the ferryman the money. Everything seemed all right until he couldn't get the little ferry off the bank, a couple of the fellows around me got off to help push and the German guard on the ferry was also helping to push.

Fig.5e The spot where I pushed the boat off the bank of the river (taken after the war)

I didn't go to help until a woman started looking at me, more or less saying why I didn't get off and help? I decided to help. The only place to push was next to the German guard. He said something to me. I answered back in Dutch, "Ja, Ja", which seemed OK! I guess there was no way he would think a Canadian airman would be pushing a boat off the river bank along side him. Little did he know there were seven of us. After crossing the river we had an hour or so to go to come to Amerogen. Roger and I were taken into the house of Cornelissen. There we found a husband and his wife who couldn't speak English, but their sixteen year old teenage daughter could speak a little Her name was Nellie. She must have impressed me, as I remember her very clearly. We were taken up to a big attic where Roger and I stayed, while two of the other fellows, were taken to the family Esveld and the three others in the family of Hoogland. Our hosts were farmers and had enough food put away to feed us. We were expected to leave in a day or so.

Fig.5f Dirk   *Fig.5g Dirk after the*
Jan. 2 1944   *war in his Army uniform*

Fig.5h House of Cornelissen

Fig.5i Mr. and Mrs. Cornelissen

Fig.5j Nellie (only 16 at this time)

There was also a Jewish fellow and a Dutchman hiding in the same house as us. We taught the Jewish fellow how to play cribbage. He had never played it before. We had played it night and day during our period of hiding in Holland. He would sit and figure out every card and I don't think we ever beat him, once he learned the game. That bothered us to no end. A couple of days before Christmas, we had a chance to write another letter, which a courier was going to take across the lines. Couriers were Dutchmen who went alone at night through the lines taking messages and bringing messages back. It was a very dangerous task with lots of challenges but only a few got caught. Letters I wrote to Ginger, and Roger wrote to his mother in Courtney, BC were by passed on by courier. He wrote his mother, "we are playing cribbage together and you must contact Bob's mother." He added, "Everything is OK," not thinking that this letter would place us together. We were not taking much care about what we said because we expected to be back in England in the very near future. Christmas came and it was like any other day. The Dutch were so fed up with the Germans and the war that they ignored it. Roger and I sat in the front room most of the day and played cribbage. After playing a few games, we tried to sing some Christmas tunes, but neither one of us had very much of a voice, so it was not very successful. We then decided to go up to see Wilf Berry and Marcel Briere. They had a Christmas tree for the little girl who lived in the house. Wilf, who was the "Sergeant Major," had a Sten gun wrapped up under the tree so we could take it with us. It was quite a Christmas present! We next walked over to visit Gri, Harvey and Louis and then walked back to Cornelissens. We were a little fed up because we expected to cross the lines over Christmas. It became quite nerve racking, as we were very close to the launching sites used by the Germans to fire over to England. The rockets were very noisy and never seemed to stop. They were launched day and night. That was Hitler's secret weapon going off and my Christmas of 1944.

We met a couple of British paratroopers from the Arnhem airborne drop. They were also getting fed up and were very anxious to get back. Hundreds of them had been hanging around for months and the Dutch could not look after them all properly. I had been very lucky as I had been in Holland all by myself for a long time and had great places to stay! I had met some very good people. I had been able to get about easily but there with the large numbers of airborne soldiers on the loose, most of the evaders had to be in hiding all the time. It seemed very strange that we were a wandering around, visiting friends, only a few miles from the front lines. Food was really becoming very scarce and hard to find, as so many of the soldiers from the failed parachute drop at Arnhem were concentrated in the south where we now were. W e met an English Private, a Sergeant and a Captain, who was a Medical Doctor Paratrooper, who were also going to go with us.

New Year's Eve came and it was very quiet. W e sat up until twelve o'clock, listening to the buzz bombs going over to England, then wished each other a Happy New Year. The little Jewish fellow wouldn't sit up with us, so we sneaked up to his bed at twelve, lifted the blankets up and poured a little cold water on him, to wish him a Happy New Year. He did not appreciate it and it was sort of a mean trick, but one has to have a little fun once in a while.

The man in charge of the Underground in this area and Dirk were still finishing their plan to get us back. They had arranged with a German soldier to let us through where he was going to be on guard, but he was sent on leave or was posted some place else. So everything had changed and new plans had to be made.

The Air Ministry sent a letter to the RCAF on Dec. 24th, 1944, and the RCAF in turn sent a letter to my mother and my wife on Dec. 26th, 1944. Registered, secret _and confidential_ . They had received a secret message that I had been safe in hiding as of July. My wife and my mother had heard nothing since June when I was shot down. They still didn't know if I was alive or not.

OUR FILE....... E.133074 ...... (R.O.4)
REF. YOUR ....
DATED . ...

ROYAL CANADIAN AIR FORCE

R E G I S T E R E D
S E C R E T
C O N F I D E N T I A L
A I R   M A I L

OTTAWA, Canada, 26th December, 1944.

Mr. C.A. Porter,
3406 Imperial Street,
New Westminster, B.C.

Dear Mr. Porter:

      The Royal Canadian Air Force Casualties Officer, Overseas, has advised me that a secret message has been received, concerning your son, Flight Sergeant Robert Edward Porter, previously reported missing on Active Service.

      It is advised that your son is known to have been safe and in hiding in enemy occupied territory July 7th, and no information concerning him has been received from any source, subsequent to that date. On no account whatever must this information be communicated to anyone. Although grave anxiety is now felt for his safety in view of the lapse of time during which no information has been received, in order to ensure every possible chance of your son's safety as well as others and those that may be assisting them, this news is not to be disclosed even to friends.

      You may rest assured that as soon as further advice is released to these Headquarters it will be communicated to you immediately.

      May I offer you my sincere sympathy in your continued anxiety.

                    Yours sincerely,

                    R.C.A.F. Casualty Officer,
                    for Chief of the Air Staff.

R.C.A.F. G. 32B
M9M—1-44 (2723)

Fig.5k Letter of December 26th saying I was seen July 7th

Chapter Six

January to Concentration

On January first we were told that we were leaving the next day. According to the plan, we were to go by bicycle to Opheusden about ten kilometres away only a few miles from the front lines. From there we were to walk to an old brick-yard, down by the River Waal, very close to the front line. We would then pass through the German lines to no man's land, cross a bridge and, when dark, cross over the canal. A Canadian army patrol was to meet us and guide us through the Allied' lines. This seemed simple but a little frightening, as I was not trained in army life and did not really know what to expect. I told the guys that I'd rather be up in the sky dropping bombs than down here catching them. We left on bicycles, early in the evening, and rode about ten or twelve miles to Opheusden and left our bicycle there, I don't know who picked up all the bicycles as we seemed to be changing or leaving them all the time. We walked a few miles through the German rear lines to the old barn like building , in the brick yard, where everyone was to meet. The foreman of the brickyard, Leo Wels,

141

was to hide us until the nightfall. There were the seven of us plus the three paratroopers. Later another five plus our guides came along, making nineteen of us. No one introduced anyone. As usual, what you did not know, you could not tell. We waited until dark before leaving. We were travelling really light, (I can't even remember having any food with us). There was ice all around and it was very cold.

Fig. 6a Brick yard we met on January 2, 1945

I was planning on staying pretty close to Roger or Wilf, as they knew more of this army life than I did, and I knew them better than the others as we had lived together and hid upstairs together in the attic.

When it got dark we started off, nineteen of us including Dirk and two other guides. We got to the bridge safely and waited around for a while, but no Canadian patrol showed up. Finally, we decided we'd go it on our own. After walking a few more miles, we ran into a German patrol and all of us scattered, then lying low until they had passed by.

We managed to assemble again but found that we had lost our two Dutch guides. It's pretty easy to lose someone when it is very dark and you can't talk because you do not know how close the Germans were. However, we had to go on. We stayed pretty close to the river, and sneaked past quite a few German outposts, so close to them that we could hear them talking. For someone like me, who had never been in the army, I was having to learn very fast.

Started here at Amerongen Jan 2nd

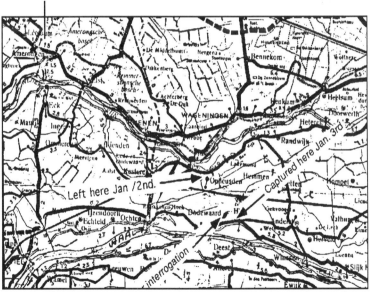

Fig. 6b Map of area where we were captured

There was no time to be frightened but I guess I was, so I tried to make it a game. I felt sure the Germans would hear us, as there was so much ice and it was breaking up and making quite a bit of noise.

However, we passed the outposts and didn't see any more for quite awhile. We were on the edge of the flooded low lands, which the Germans had flooded at Arnhem, when the British landed there. It had later frozen over, then thawed, and it was now in an in-between state.

We ran into lots of drowned cattle, all bloated up. It was an awful feeling to fall on a bloated, slimy, slippery dead cow in the dark. We didn't know what they were at first, it was so very dark! It seemed a great waste when so many were going hungry.

We walked further. It was about ten o'clock when we came to another old brick yard. Where were we? No one seemed to know. The Dutchmen we had lost were our main guides and the others, who were with us going across on Underground business, didn't know much more than we did. With the one compass we had, we decided to head south. We knew we had gone through what was called "no man's land" and felt we were pretty close to the British lines, that we only had to go a few more miles. We left and headed down the road, going in a roughly southern direction. We were sure we had to cross the river but we were hoping to find some Allied troops on this side of the river Waal.

We eventually came to another cross road and now didn't know which way to go. As we crossed the road, a fellow on a bicycle came along. We weren't going to stop him as we didn't know whether he was British or German. We let him go by but he saw us. As we started to go in the same direction, suddenly there was a shout and machine gun fire. All hell broke loose along the road, and we all ran in every direction. Now we were really scattered. I lost track of Roger and found myself with Wilf Berry, being a sergeant major in the Army, he gave me a very quick course on army life. When he said run, I ran.

The Germans became very excited. They would fire a big flare in the air and then shoot at anything they saw or anything that moved. Wilf would say "dive" and I would dive. Sometimes we were on the ice, sometimes in mud or in water six inches to a foot deep. However, when you are being shot at, you get down very fast and lay very still. Wilf had been shot in the arm so we made up a bit of a sling and kept going. We ran very fast to try and get out of this area. Wilf still had his Sten gun but there was no time to use it.

In a couple of hours, things quieted down. We knew that they had shot a couple of our guys and we did not know what happened to the others. Some were captured, and maybe they thought that was all there were. I was wearing a pair of light oxfords, but I lost them in the mud and ice. Coming across an old fruit shed, we decided to hold up there for the night, hoping that things might look better in the morning. At this stage, Wilf and I were not a very active pair, he with his wounded arm and me with no shoes in the ice and mud. It had been a long night.

The night of January second was a very long night! Here we were, Wilf and I, hiding most of the night in an old shed, on the flood plains of the river Waal, cold, wet and hungry. We could hear voices in the distance but could not tell if they were German or

English. Since we had gone through the German lines, we were now sitting in the middle of it all and there was no going back. It was unbelievable! W e were so close to the German Posts that we could hear them talking. Gads, if I let my mind go a little I would think I was in a movie. We knew we were in no man's land, and we were at a very low ebb in life. This was real army life. I was trained to fly, not to fight down here.

The shed where were in, had some apples that had been stored in a barrel before the invasion. W e were hungry and we tried eating them but they had been frozen and thawed out and were awful! Then we looked around and found a barrel of sauerkraut. I had never eaten sauerkraut at home, but I'd eaten it a few times at my sister Jean's place as her husband, Alfred, was Polish. I had just begun acquiring a bit of a taste for it. So into the barrel we went. It was not very good, but we ate some, although it was really rotten! I don't think I ever enjoyed eating sauerkraut again!

Wilf's arm was really hurting now and my feet felt as if they were half frozen. The shoes I had been wearing were an old pair of oxfords. There was no use wearing a good pair as I thought I would be able to buy a new pair in London the next day! I had taken the heel off, cut a hollow out, put my identity disks in the hole and put the heel back on again. So, losing my shoes meant I had lost my identification. That was not good! It also wasn't good that we had civilian clothes on, which is illegal for servicemen in war time.

We had to make a decision, we couldn't stay in the shed and the river was too wide to get across. Wilf couldn't swim with a bullet in his arm and I didn't know how. I was never much for water and never learned to swim until I was 40 years old. I was a slow learner as far as swimming was concerned. We made a decision to head toward the voices. We soon found out that it was the wrong way to go. It was the German camp. We were very depressed as we were so sure we would be in London for the New Year and were now very apprehensive of what would happen to us. W e were in civilian clothes. They had chased us all night. We knew what they did to the Underground people when they were captured. We were so close to freedom yet so far away.

The German troops weren't very pleased with us as they had been up most of the night, looking for us. Wilf had left his Sten Gun in the shed but they found it afterwards. They thought we were in the Dutch Underground because we were also in civilian clothes. Some of them had been hurt in the fight the night before and we learned that four or five of our group had been killed. We found out later that only three of the nineteen made it to the other side, but they were in very bad shape as they had to swim the frozen canal. I'm sure I would have died doing that, even if I were able to swim. The successful ones were, Captain Roger Schjelderup, Sgt. Gri, and Private Hardy who were all very experienced soldiers. They had landed on D-Day and had fought through France and Belgium.

It was fortunate that our captors were from the regular army, the Wermacht although they were not very pleased with us, I don't think they knew what to do with us. How often would they have captured military personnel in civilian clothes? They had every right to shoot us, but instead they gave me a pair of wooden shoes, which was a God-send. Walking on bare feet is very tough at the best of times, but in the winter it's really bad. The wooden shoes were very awkward to walk in, but a lot better then nothing and that was all I had to walk in for the next three months. They also gave us a bowl of hot soup which tasted really good right then. I guess anything would have tasted good at that moment. I often wonder if a group of our army personnel who had been up half the night chasing a bunch of Underground and enemy in soldiers civilian clothes would have been as nice. Some army guys I talked to later said, "You were very lucky that they didn't shoot you right there."

Our nice treatment didn't last long. I guess we were a big catch for the Germans. They had caught Dutch Underground people, military personnel and they were not sure who else. The Field Army Police (Feld-Gendarmerie) soon took over the investigation. They were special police who were connected to the army, part of or similar, to the Gestapo. They were not very nice to us! I think they would have liked to have us shot right there. We saw Dirk, the Dutch guide, who had been with us. It was very sad. The Dutch Underground were treated much worse than we were. Dirk had also lost his shoes in the mud and ice, but the Germans did not give him any shoes and his feet were bleeding badly. He had some old rags wrapped around them. They had also beaten him up severely. We had to totally ignore him as it wouldn't have done either of us any good to have recognised each other. It was very hard. I always thought he must have lost his feet or died in a concentration camp. I saw him in the next couple of weeks off and on, but then never saw him again. Louis, Marcel, Harvey, and the doctor from the Army all showed up, but we didn't see any of the others.

They began to interrogate us, very seriously. We all stuck to our story, as previously arranged. We did not know each other and we had never met before last night. That way, we did not have to worry about the other person's story. Each one made up their own story and had to stick to it. The Geneva Convention set out how prisoners of war were to be treated. The Germans and the Allies stuck close to it, although the Japanese and the Russians did not. However, civilian political prisoners were not covered by the Geneva Convention, and that is why the concentration camps were so horrible. They were filled with civilian and political prisoners. We were only obliged to give our name, rank and serial number and we tried to stick to it. They told us many times that, as we were captured in civilian clothes and armed, that we were classified as spies so not protected by the Geneva Convention, so they could shoot us. We were kept apart most of the time but we would be put together for some reason every once in a while. We were too frightened to talk about anything, in case they were listening or had microphones around. It was scary!

We were only kept near the front line for a day or so, then Wilf, Louis, Harvey, Marcel Briere, the Army Doctor and myself were taken to Arnhem. The Dutch fellows were taken to a concentration camp. It is very hard to imagine the harsh treatment that the political prisoners had to endure. We had it very tough but they had it much worse. Whatever is written or shown in the movies about that time, doesn't describe nearly how bad it really was. It is hard to imagine how hideous and horrible people can be, especially the Gestapo and the SS. There was also a group of Dutch civilians, who were German sympathisers (I think they were sadists to begin with) when the Germans took over Holland the NSB jumped on the band wagon, expecting the Germans to win. They were arrogant and cruel to their own countrymen, such as the Underground, who opposed very much the German occupation.

In Arnhem we were held in a house that the Germans had taken over after the paratroopers came. The windows and doors were barred, and there were security guards for each cell for it. My guard was a German airman who was not a SS type, and he was fed up with the war. He wasn't flying because they didn't have any aeroplanes to fly. Hitler and some of his generals had a big disagreement about defence, especially Rommel and Hitler. Hitler was the Supreme Commander so he decided to cut the Air Force and spend their budget on the V-2 Rocket (Revenge Weapon #2), a self-propelled Rocket which they could guide to a target. It was not very accurate. Hitler and his close advisers called it their secret weapon and had great hopes that it would win the war.

The Germans produced a lot of propaganda, continuing the attitude that they were going to win the war, right up to the very end. So, here was my guard, an experienced pilot, doing duty as a security guard and he didn't like it. We used to compare stories about bombing each other's country; he had bombed England and I had bombed Germany. He was very nice and we talked a lot, but I never said anything that I didn't want the interrogators to know.

Our interrogators were another species altogether. By this time we had attracted the more senior interrogators and they were much meaner. As soon as I gave my name, rank and number, they knew who I was. They told me when I had been shot down and where my crew was buried. They knew I had been on the loose for seven months. They knew what squadron I was from and where we were bombing the night we were shot down. However, their main purpose was to know where the Dutch Underground had taken care of me and by whom. The Dutch Underground was a thorn in their side, which is why they put them in concentration camps and treated them cruelly. They shot many and all were tortured. As prisoners we were fed very little; they had the starvation diet down to a science. They gave us just enough so we wouldn't starve to death. A cup of ersatz coffee for breakfast, a bowl of watery cabbage soup for lunch and sometimes a piece of very black sourdough bread at night. They would interrogate us at any time, day or night.

The doctor, a British Army medical officer who was captured with us, was also being held in the same house as us. He was tough and kept himself perfectly dressed. Only an Englishman could keep himself so clean under these circumstances. He slept on a straw mat and at night he would lay his pants under them so they would keep a press. He had a double guard as he was always trying to escape, whether it was practical or not. He was determined to keep as many Germans busy as possible. He had a little more freedom to do things than we had, as he was a major, and had been captured in uniform and with ID. The Germans were not threatening to shoot him and treated him as a proper POW. It was his duty to try and escape.

I had been in Holland for the longest time and could guess what the Germans were saying, as the language is similar to Dutch. Therefore I was chosen as spokesman. Each room had a small coke stove in it and my job was to go around and clean out the ashes. The advantage to this was that most of the guards couldn't speak or understand English. I would pretend to talk to the guard but really would be talking to the fellow in the room. In this way we kept in contact and told each other about what was going on, but one had to be very careful. We saw how they had treated Dirk and we didn't want the same treatment.

We were guarded by the Wermacht. These were regular German soldiers who were fed up with the war and had never been Nazi fanatics. Even they were afraid of the SS and the Gestapo. However, we were interrogated by SS troops who wore a black uniform including skull and cross bones emblem on their hat. They also wore long black leather coats and I still have strong feelings whenever I see a long black coat. The feeling still goes through me today. They also wore a big red swastika on their arm. They were hard-core Nazis and had a lot of power, taking their orders directly from Himmler.

We were also interrogated by the Gestapo. They wore civilian clothes and were even worse. I think everybody was afraid of them. The Gestapo seemed to have power over everyone, but there also appeared to be quite a lot of power struggles between themselves and the SS. The Gestapo wanted information on the Underground movement while the SS concentrated more on the military. The Secrete Service, who interrogated us after the Field Army Police (Feld-Gendarmerie), we never saw again. I think they were the secret police within the army.

Wilf's arm was seen by a doctor here. He took the bullet out and put his arm in a cast, and used a paper bandage. I guess that was all that they had. You would never guess what a great advantage that paper bandage was! We had nothing to smoke but we would gather up cigarette butts, pull some of the paper bandage out of the dressing on Wilf's arm and use it to roll a cigarette. As time went on, Wilf's arm got thinner with the lack of food and, with us pulling the bandage out of his cast, his cast was eventually just flopping around, very loose. I can't remember how we got it off, I think it fell off!

We began to be interrogated more and more, at all different times of the day. We were asked the same questions, over and over. Our interrogators would then check back to what we had said the time before. At times they would eat a large meal in front of us and do different things like that to increase the stress. They loved to blow smoke in our face as we never had any cigarettes. I was very surprised that these SS often had American cigarettes. We were pushed around quite a bit, whacked across the head a few times, but we were never tortured like the civilians were.

They kept referring to us as spies and threatened to shoot us many times. They always let us know that we had no rights under the Geneva Convention. They would talk about my crew and my squadron. They would ask about things that had happened in 419 Squadron such as where I flew from and asked questions about other crews who had been shot down. They would talk about the pub near the squadron, trying to get a conversation going. We treated it as a big jigsaw puzzle, and searching for all the little pieces to fit into it. They would try to talk about Canada and where I was from. They tried to get you relaxed, as if it didn't matter what you said, as small as it may be. We always apologised and told them that we could only give them our name, rank and number. They would then yell at us, "You have no rights," and get really mad. However, I told them the same story, over and over.

My story was that I didn't know where I had landed in Holland, that I had met a farmer and lived in his barn. I had lived by myself, never talked to anybody and never knew where I was. I would have to go over the exact description of the room I had slept in and the barn, everything down to the last detail. The farmer never spoke English, I couldn't speak

Dutch and he was too afraid to have me meet any-one. I memorised this story. Every night I would go over and over it. I couldn't miss one detail, each time I told my story it had to be exactly the same. I would make a visual picture of the farmyard and the room in the barn where I slept. I went over it so often that I began to believe it myself. They never believed it and let me know in a very violent way. Often by a whack on the head and telling me that I could be shot. W e figured that as long as we didn't talk they wouldn't shoot us. If we did talk, many good Dutch people would have been shot as well as ourselves, as then they would have nothing to keep us alive for.

My mother had given me a wrist watch when I joined the Air Force. It was the most valuable thing I had. Every mother should give their child a good watch when they leave home. I could always hock it and get $5.00 when I was broke. The German guards also wanted it, so I would hide it in many places. A few times they tried to take it, but I would pretend that they just wanted to know the time. If they got too ag-gressive, I would say, "Come see Officer". I kept this watch all through the war and then lost it digging a ditch in Langley, when I was an apprentice plumber a year after the war.

The SS and the Gestapo were very well organised. They had an excellent cross reference system in their intelligence. Once, I was being interrogated at three or four o'clock in the morning and the interrogator was big and as mean as usual. I had gone over my story three or four times with him. He questioned m e on many points, on the way I had been living in Holland and especially who I had talked to. I knew he was after something, but I couldn't figure out what. He kept shuffling this bunch of papers on his desk and I couldn't see what they were! I remembered I had a blank piece of paper in my pocket when I was captured and I had made up a story about it. I was concerned that I might have written something on the page before and that the pencil had marked through to the next page. Maybe they had some way of reading that. I couldn't remember the story I had told him, about what I thought might be on the paper, but at the time I thought it sounded good. I couldn't think of anything else to say. He wasn't very pleased with that story. Suddenly he reached over his desk, gave me a real hard blow on the ear, called me "a Goddam liar," and just glared at me. I didn't have time to duck as it came as a complete surprise. He was looking down at the papers on his desk, moved one over and there was a letter that I had written months ago. It was a letter to my mother written on tissue paper. I had drilled a hole down the body of a wooden comb, rolled the note up, put it in the hole, made a plug and plugged the hole. I refinished the comb and gave it to an Underground courier who was going across the German lines, with information for the Allies. He'd said, "I will mail it at British Head-quarters when I get there." We never heard from him again but I figured he had made it. I had said in the letter that I had been playing crib all day with a Roger Schjelderup, from Courtney BC, and could she please phone his mother to tell her that we were both alive and well?" My story to the Germans had always been the same, that I had lived alone in a barn, on a farm, and saw no one. The interrogator was wild and I thought he was going to come after me again. Lucky for me he was tired and cranky, as it was the middle of the night. He physically kicked me, threw me out of the office and bellowed for the guard to take me back to my cell.

The courier must have been caught because they found the comb with all the other papers. If we were smart enough to put the letter in the comb, they were smart enough to find it. I didn't have much time to think about what had happened to the courier, but I was certain it wasn't very nice. He would have been severely tortured for information and then shot or put in a concentration camp. They would slap such prisoners across the head and ears until they bled, then they broke their fingers one by one. This would be kept up hour after hour, with no let up. They were given almost no food and, if lucky, slept on a cement floor. The Dutch Underground accepted and worked for their country with no pay, no recognition and as no one knew what they were doing, in most cases ended up without any thanks. I will always have enormous respect for the Dutch people and I wouldn't be here today if it wasn't for them.

I had a lot to think about when I got back to my cell. I decided I was going to stick to my story and only change it by adding Roger into it. I didn't have a clue where Roger was. He may have been caught and was being held someplace else, or he may have been killed along with the others, or by some miracle maybe he may have gotten through to the British lines. I was going to go with the premise he wasn't around and make up my own story. I only had one more interrogation with this interrogator and although he didn't believe me, it was the only story I had and I stuck to it. Arnhem was close to the front line, so they only kept us in this location for a week or so. We were then moved by truck to a big prison in Utrecht called "Wolvenplein Prison" where we were very well guarded, one for each of us. They knew I had spent the last seven months around there, someplace, and that I knew a little of the language. They were not taking any chance on us making a run for it, but we never got the chance. The prison was run by the German SS. It held only political prisoners, Dutch civilians who had been caught doing something against the Germans. Ans Middelkoop was a prisoner here at the same time but I did not know that until after the war, she had a very bad time. Her son Kees had been taken away from her. I believe if anyone was arrested for other crimes they were sent directly to Germany to work in the forced labour camps. Later, an older man was put in with me who couldn't speak a word of English but, because I was there first, I had the bunk and he had to sleep on the floor. He often thought I could understand him and would talk on and on in Dutch. I guess he was also frightened and had no one else to talk to.

Fig. 6c The Jail in Utrecht I was in Jan. 1945

Some days we would be let out of our cells for ten minutes or so and were allowed to walk around a fenced-in yard, but not for very long. It was a wired-in area about fifteen feet long and six feet wide, having brick walls on two sides, and wire mesh at the ends and over the top as a roof. This was our exercise yard. We were interrogated most days and nights and the interrogators were getting meaner and meaner. I never saw the other prisoners and didn't know if they were still there or not. I felt alone in the world. There was a Dutch worker cleaning up around the prison. He spoke good English and would talk to me sometimes while he was working. I thought I would take a chance and talk to him. He said, "I know a few people in the Underground, maybe I can get you some help." I replied that I don't know anyone's name or where they lived. "Would you ask the ones you know if anyone knows me? " I asked, hoping that someone I had met would get the message to Rakers. I continued, "If they do, would they pass the word around that I'm here and I'd really like to get out?"

Fig.6d Exercise area. We may have 10 minutes a day here

I was getting anxious thinking that maybe they would shoot me, as they claimed they had the right to. There would often be shooting in the next room and they would say, "See!" They had threatened me enough times. The only way they might be able to get me out was to send me a "Diphtheria sandwich." I had seen Rakers do it before. Rakers would make arrangements with Slim, who was an orderly in the hospital to take diphtheria germs from a patients' throat and put them in a vial. Next Rakers would make a sandwich and put the germs in it. He would then send the sandwich to the prisoners they wanted to get out, hoping he would get diphtheria. The Germans were very afraid of this disease and would send the prisoners to a hospital. The Underground could get him out once he was in the hospital. It sounds drastic but these were tough times and I was worried that the captors would turn nastier and nastier.

I could stand up on the window sill and look out the little window. I was sure I could see De Baai's house, the first people I lived with in Utrecht. It seemed so close but so far away. The cells were very small and bare. A cot was on one side and there was a bucket in the corner. No washing facilities at all. I had been imprisoned for at least three weeks and had not yet seen a place to wash.

One day, after a week or so, I was taken out of my cell as if I was going for interrogation or just to the exercise yard, but instead I was put in a truck with some others. We didn't have to pack or pick up anything as we had no possessions, absolutely nothing. There were a couple of guards with machine guns and I don't think they would have hesitated to use them. Wilf, Louis, Harvey and Marcel were there. This was the first I had seen of them since we were brought from Wolvenplein. It gave me a great feeling to know I was no longer totally alone. The German guards shouted something nasty and we agreed it had meant, "No talking," so we didn't. Some of them never seemed to have a sense of humour.

We headed out of Utrecht, towards Hilversum, right past Raker's house in Groenekan where I had lived for seven months. Wilf and the others had lived up the road at Bilthoven. We dared not look at the house or even at each other. The thought ran through my head that, maybe they knew something and they were just testing us. We kept going and nothing came of it. The truck we were in was fuelled by some sort of wood gas with a wood burner in the back. They had to keep it burning, to produce the gas to keep us going. At this time the Germans didn't have much gasoline and what they did have was kept for the army at the front lines. This wood burning truck was their transportation. The Germans were constantly looking around, watching for Allied fighter bombers. They came from out of nowhere. If we saw one, we just jumped out of the truck and ran like hell, with the guards right behind us.

We drove for a few hours, then stopped and were taken into a big building with a lot of Dutch civilian prisoners, all standing in rows, who also seemed to have just been brought in. They were being guarded by the NSB. One of the prisoners fell over, talked or did something I'm not sure what. Whatever it was, the guards reacted very quickly. Two of the NSB started to shout and yell. They pushed the Dutchman out of the room and when they brought him back a little while later, he had been beaten up severely, with his eyes half closed and his face swollen. It was awful, but it made us think and watch what we were doing. We decided that there was no sense of humour here!

We had no idea why we were there but late that afternoon we were loaded back into the truck along with a few of the Dutch civilians. Now we had both the German guards and the NSB. They were shouting a lot, so we sat quietly. We hadn't had anything to eat since the small piece of bread from the night before,

and it didn't look like we were going to get anything to eat today. This wasn't the time to talk about our rights. They kept saying, "At the next place there will be something to eat," but we never did get anything that day.

Chapter Seven

Concentration Camp to POW

We arrived at a rough looking place, a very well guarded concentration camp. I believe that was the Kruisberge at Doetinchem. It was late at night and very dark. We were tossed in a cell with a concrete floor but without our piece of bread. This often happened, you just didn't get fed. There was nothing in the room. It was black, cold and damp. It was the end of January and they were not going to waste heat on us. I was put in the same cell as Wilf. We half sat and half lay on the floor hard and cold. As we got thinner and lost all the fat around our behind and hips, the cement floor got harder and harder. We heard a noise all night and didn't know whether it was mice, rats or something else. It went, "tap, tap, tap". There was no way we could figure out what it was, but in the morning we found out. It was so damned cold and muggy, our breath was condensing on the ceiling and some big drops were dropping on the hard cement floor!

When I was on Squadron, before I was shot down, the dentist had been working on my teeth and had put a bunch of temporary fillings in them. The night I got shot down, with the shock of it all, my temporary fillings had come out. My teeth were really beginning to bother me now. Wilf used to put his false teeth on the floor and say, "Ache you buggers ache." This did not help me much, except it put a little humour in our lives. I couldn't go to the guards to ask for something for a tooth ache, since they would have just laughed.

We just had to sit on the cement floor and talk. There were no books or cards. Imagine a concrete cell, concrete floor and a bucket in the corner and nothing else.

As the days went on, we ran out of things to talk about. We used to divide the day up by different subjects, with food the main topic. We could always find something to talk about on that subject, but it did not help our hunger. We would talk about what food we would eat when we got home. Another favourite topic was about the little house we wanted after the war, if we ever got out of this place. A house with a white picket fence, flower garden and vegetables. What would we plant? This would sometimes take a couple of hours. Women often got into the conversation. There were lots of things we would talk about, but always pleasant things. Neither one of us was interested in politics at that time, so it didn't come up. We would talk about before the war and before I was shot down. However, we never talked about Holland or about knowing each other before being captured. We were very careful about that, feeling we were being watched or listened to. If we were given two pieces of something to eat, we always ate it right away. Wilf used to say, "It's better to be lit-

tle bit filled once than hungry twice." The odd time
we would try to talk about religion but neither one of
us had very much religion in us to start with. If there
was a God, how could he let these horrible things go
on? They had been going on for many years. We just
couldn't understand how the Pope and the other religious leaders could let these horrible things happen.

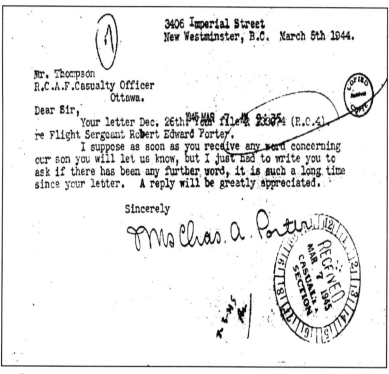

**Fig.7a March 5 1945. My mother wrote to Ottawa
trying to find out something**

ROYAL CANADIAN AIR FORCE

OVERSEAS HEADQUARTERS
73-77, Oxford Street, London, W. 1.

24th February, 1945.

S E C R E T
The Secretary,
Department of National Defence for Air,
Lisgar Building, Ottawa, Ontario, CANADA

Attention: R.O.4.
R.113074 F/Sgt. R.E. Porter.
1. Further to my message E.664 December 1944, it is advised that Canadian Military Headquarters here have forwarded the following statement by Captain Vilhelm Roger Schjelderup and Sgt. Gri, A Canadian Army personnel who recently returned to the UK, regarding the above mentioned airman:
"He was shot down in the North of Holland in July. He was last seen on the night of January 2nd when he was shot while crossing the ice. He was not seen since. He was in civilian clothes at the time."
2. Upon receipt of the above, Captain Schjelderup and Sgt. Gri were contacted with a view to obtaining further details, and the following statements were received:
Captain Schjelderup states:
"On the night of 2nd/3rd January 1945, F/ Sgt. Porter, myself and others set out to cross through the lines to freed Holland. The party was badly shot up, and on the second shooting, F/Sgt. Porter and others panicked. I last saw them crashing out across the ice in a badly flooded area under fire from three German machine gun posts. I never saw them again. I did not see F/Sgt. Porter shot. There is a slight chance of him having been taken prisoner. He was dressed in civilian clothes and his only means of identification was one of his identity discs which he was wearing at the time."
Sgt. Gri stated: -
"At approximately 23:30 hours on 2nd January 1945, I was one of 13 people making their way back to the British lines between the Maas and the Rhine Rivers. We were fired on, and all took cover. With the exception of myself and two others in the party, the remainder moved off, and we were unable to locate them after that.
Sgt. Porter, R., of the R.C.A.F. was a member of that party."
3. No other information has been received regarding this airman.
4 The above information will be forwarded to this airman's wife on the 10th March, as per attached letter, if no further information is received by that time.

E Gibb F/L

For Air Officer Commanding
For J.S.Harris Wing Commander, in Chief,
R.C.A.F. Overseas.

Fig.7b Feb. 24th (A copy of a letter) from the RCAF to Ottawa, but not to my mother

How could the people in England, Canada, United States plus all the other Allied countries be praying to God for their victory and all the Germans praying to the same God, through the same religions, for their victory? Maybe we were stupid but it didn't make any sense to us. Both sides couldn't be right. The days were long and the nights even longer, as this was February. It got dark very early and daylight seemed a long time coming. We had no lights or candles. I don't think the Germans had many candles themselves and practically no electricity. Although even if they had any, I don't think they would have shared them with us, since we were still very low on the totem pole of life. We had a little window. We could just manage to look out of it if we stood on our toes. Once, when we heard a noise outside our window we found a bunch of girls out in the exercise yard. We knocked on the window and waved. We wrote on the glass, but I can't remember what with, "We are Canadians" and waved at them again. We thought we were quite bright. It didn't take very much to give us a little thrill. They didn't wave back as they were prisoners too and I guess they were frightened. Pretty soon guards came around and painted the outside of our window with black paint. So that was the last of our socialising. We couldn't look out the little window to see if it was even raining or not. But maybe we gave some of the women prisoners something to talk about. They would be wondering what Canadians were doing in a concentration camp, since only civilians were imprisoned there. We had so little food. Our diet was a cup of ersatz coffee (a poor imitation of coffee) in the morning, a small piece of black bread for lunch and a bowl of watery cabbage soup for supper. That was what we were suppose to get, but sometimes they would forget or just didn't come! With this lack of food, we became very weak. If we got up too fast, we would pass out. We would have to get up slowly, sometimes hanging on to something, otherwise we would pass out and wake up laying on the floor.

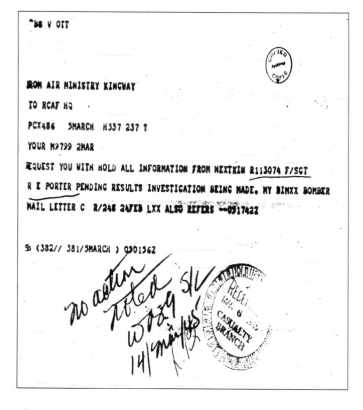

Fig. 7c Air Ministry to RCAF "Withhold all information" on R. E. Porter

AIR MINISTRY

73-77, Oxford Street, London, W.I.

10th March 1945.

<u>CAN/ Re 133074 / P.4./ CAS/C.4.</u>

Dear Mrs. Porter,

Further to my letter of the 21st December, 1944, I wish to inform you that further information has been received concerning your husband, Flight Sergeant Robert Edward Porter, but which, unfortunately, does not establish whether he is now alive.

A report has been received to the effect that your husband was with a party of Allied servicemen who were making their way back to Allied territory on the night of the 2nd /3rd January 1945. The party was subjected to considerable fire by the Germans; at this point the party was separated and your husband and others were last seen running across the ice in a badly flooded area.

A further report has reached us which states that two members of the party were killed. No further information has been received concerning your husband, and in view of the lapse of time, grave consideration must be given to the possibility that he may have lost his life at that time.

You may be assured that immediately upon receipt of further news, you will be informed.

Please accept my deepest sympathy with you during this trying time.

Yours sincerely,

E J Figg H/L

for *(J S. Harris),Wing Commander, for Air Officer Commanding in chief, R.C.A.F. Overseas.*

Mrs. R.E. Porter
18, Lewyn Helyg Nantybwch,.
Tredegar, Mon.

Fig.7d (A copy of the Letter) March 10th from Air Ministry to my wife. Saying I was with a party of soldier January 2nd 1945

ADDRESS REPLY TO:

THE S. _ .ETARY,

DEPARTMENT OF NATIONAL DEFENCE FOR AIR,

OTTAWA, ONTARIO.

OUR FILE R.153074(R04)

REF. YOUR

DATED

ROYAL CANADIAN AIR FORCE

OTTAWA, Canada, March 16th, 1945.

C O N F I D E N T I A L

A I R   M A I L

Mrs. C.A. Porter,
3406 Imperial Street,
New Westminster,
British Columbia.

Dear Mrs. Porter:

I wish to acknowledge your letter of recent date concerning your son, Flight Sergeant Robert Edward Porter.

I am indeed sorry but since my letter dated December 26th, 1944, no further information concerning your son has been received. Your very great anxiety for further word is fully realised and I wish to assure that just as soon as it is received you will be at once advised.

May I again extend my sincere sympathy during this anxious period of waiting.

Yours sincerely,

R.C.A.F. G. 322
30M—1-44 (2778)
H.Q. 86-G-HB

R.C.A.F. Casualty Officer,
for Chief of the Air Staff.

Fig.7f March 16th 1945 letter from Ottawa. No news from her letter

They knew with this diet, we would just exist and that was all. We did not have anything like bathroom privileges. We had a bucket in the corner of the cell and that was it! It was almost two months now since I had my clothes off, washed or had a bath.

I wore a zipper sweater and would keep it zippered up. I couldn't smell myself by then. I don't remember others smelling that much either. I guess it is like eating garlic; if you both eat it, you can't smell the other. They put me in solitary to think over about telling them the truth, of where I had been in Holland and what I had been doing. I was put in a black room in the basement; cement floor, no windows, no lights, not a thing in the room. You didn't know if it was day or night. If you fell asleep, you couldn't tell if you slept for five minutes or five hours. The small amount of food I got was slid under the door and came at all different times. It was also dead quiet, without a sound. As a result, I had no idea how long I was in there. I finally got out one night but was taken directly to interrogation.

The Germans liked to take prisoners to interrogation in the middle of the night, probably because that was when they would be tired, the most vulnerable to pressure, and would give in to their questions more easily. The interrogator was a big fat SS officer. He was on one side of the desk, eating a big meal. They liked to do that. He said, "You could have nice things to eat if you would co-operate with me and tell me the truth." I stuck to my story, as I hadn't any other choice. After he had eaten, he opened a big book and started writing down everything I said. Always the same questions over and over. He would try different angles, or tell me a little something, hoping I would carry on and tell him a little more. They would check in the book to see if I had given the same answers as before. Later into the night he closed the book and said, "That's all for tonight, the interrogation is over." I thought to myself "Hey! what's your new angle." He took a package of American cigarettes out of his pocket, (God knows where he got them from) and said, "Have a cigarette."

That was very unusual, so I took it. We sat there for a moment or two, smoking, and then he said, "When do you think the war will be over?" I thought for a minute. Just what should I say? Then I said to myself, "Hell why not?" It was almost the end of March. I said, "I think it will be all over by June." He just sat there and didn't say anything. Then I thought I had gone this far, so I asked, "When do think it will be over?" He sat there again, thinking for a bit and then said, "It will be over before that, it will be over by May." We sat there for a while, then he turned around to me and asked, "And who do you think will win?" I thought for a minute and thought, well there is no use being a liar about it so I said, "The Allies." We sat there for another minute, just looking at each other and I didn't have a clue what he was thinking. I thought, if he is asking me, so to hell, I am going to ask him and I said: "Who do you think will win?" Again, we sat there silently for a time. He did not seem to be in a hurry to answer. He eventually replied, "the British and the Americans will win on the battlefield, but they will never beat the Russians."

That was all that he said that night and I was taken back to my cell. That was the last time I saw him. It was the first time I had ever heard a German officer even hint that they would not win the war. These interrogators spoke perfect English. Some of them had gone to Universities in England and in the States. Funnily enough, for many years we didn't beat the Russians.

Fig. 7g German war time travel. 50 to 60 of us in a small boxcar. Jewish people packed so tight they could not sit down

Chapter Eight

To Nuremburg

We had been in the concentration camp for a couple of months but now something was going on. We noticed things changing and we now had Wermacht guards only, no SS or Gestapo. One morning we were taken out of our cells and were put in the back of a truck. "Here we go again" I thought. Wilf Berry, Louis Trainor, Marcel Briere, Harvey Swartz and myself were back together again, just the five of us. The guards had a machine gun but didn't have the toughness of the SS. We didn't know if we were being moved to another place or just out for the day. As before, there was nothing to pack, nothing to take with us, we only had the clothes on our back. W e headed towards Germany, getting farther from the Allied lines all the time. The Germans seemed a little different, especially the officers. It was, we found out from somebody that General Patton counter attacked from the south to link up with them and drive

176

the Germans back. It was later known as the "Battle of the Bulge." It was in France, in the Ardennes, where General McAuliffe, was Commanding Officer of the US 101st Airborne Division which was trapped, encircled at Bastogne, Belgium. General McAuliffe was called upon to surrender but refused. He became famous for replying "Nuts" to the German demand to surrender. Eventually the US Army broke out. All the SS, Gestapo and German Officers were called back to Berlin.

We had been driving for a few hours when we came to another camp. It was a dispersal camp. The distances in Europe are not like in Canada; in a day you can drive almost from one side of the country to the other. In this camp there were all types of uniformed prisoners, army fellows and aircrew that had just been shot down during the last few days. It was a great relief to be out of the control of the SS and the Gestapo. Things could only get better as I was now classified as a Prisoner of War, a great promotion from a civilian spy in a concentration camp. I had some hope now and could see signs that we were going to get out of this mess alive.

In this small holding camp, I was separated from Wilf and the others I had been with. No good-byes. They were shoved one way and I was pushed the other. The army was also separated from the air force. The officers were separated from the non-commissioned ranks. I never saw Wilf again until a couple of years after the war.

I was put into a hut (sort of nice, compared to the cells I had been in for the last three months). It was not the least bit fancy, very sparse, but it was better than it had been. The other prisoners were air crew, some of whom had had breakfast in England only the day before. They had just been shot down or had bailed out and were still in shock, wondering what had happened to them. They all had nice clean uniforms on, looked well-fed and everyone with a nice neat haircuts. We newcomers were welcomed with a cup of ersatz coffee and a hunk of bread.

I had still not washed or shaved. My clothes were not in very good shape and I still didn't have proper shoes, only my wooden ones. I could walk well with them now, although it had taken a lot of practice. Wooden shoes are not flexible at all, so when you lift your foot up, you have to push your toes down and raise the heel up. I got to the point I could even run with them. However, my feet were not in very good shape as they had been half frozen on the ice the night I got captured. They would have been a lot better if I had had proper shoes. As I had not changed my clothes for three months and had been wet and dry many times, I had a pungent body odour. The newly captured air crew thought that I was a Dutch civilian at first as I looked very dirty, scruffy and I stunk. They tried to kick me out of their hut but I refused to go. After being on the loose for ten months, I had learned how to look after myself!

Again, the Germans thought I could understand them so I became spokesperson. I went up, when they called, to get our food rations. I won't ever forget that! It was a bucket of cabbage, or something similar, made into a soup. It looked like it even had a bit of horse meat in it. They also gave us a hunk of German black bread. The other air crew said, "No way are we going to eat that!" They weren't hungry enough yet. So, I had all I wanted of the soup and the bread! The bread that I couldn't eat, I put in my pocket. This turned some of the guys off. The bread and the soup took a little getting used to. I understand the Germans used to make the bread months ahead, some even said, years ahead. And then they wrapped it in something, so it would keep. The bread was very heavy and black, quite different to what we were used to. It had been a long time since I had been full. The newly captured guys really thought I was something different, but it wouldn't be long until they would be ready to eat. That was the main diet the German soldiers got, black bread and cabbage soup.

All these new prisoners had packages of cigarettes with them and some still had their escape packages with little luxuries in it. Some carried a couple of chocolate bars, even razors and shaving cream. Those were real luxuries to me. They didn't realise how scarce these things were going to be, but I did! I was sort of on the scrounge and their chocolate bars tasted really great! I bummed a razor and had a good shave, which was really great and I even used their shaving cream for soap. It felt so good! I acquired a couple of packs of cigarettes, but there still was no place to bathe, nor to get clean clothes.

It was really good to be able to talk to the guys about what had happened around the world and in England over the last ten months. There was a comic in the paper; called "Jane". Everyone read "Jane". She was always getting into situations and ending up nude, but nothing the least bit crude. I am sure anyone, who was ever in England during the war would remember "Jane". There were rumours that Roosevelt was very sick, but just rumours, as that would be real bad blow to the Allies if anything happened to him! He was very tough, like Churchill. The Invasion was coming along well, but it was a tough battle all the way. The German resistance was amazing after fighting a war on at least three fronts for five years. The African front was finally over.

Mussolini in Italy was finished, and the Italians had capitulated. The Germans still had big battles going on in Russia and were taking great losses. The Russians were advancing on Berlin at the same pace the Allies were going across France, Belgium and Holland. Both the Russians and the Allies wanted to take Berlin. The SS were fighting to the last man. Their belief in winning the war was unbelievable, right to the very last.

I was now a real POW. I was beyond the control of the SS and Gestapo. According to the Geneva Convention, there were things we should have been allowed, which I couldn't demand before. The problem was, the Germans didn't have anything to offer by now. A lot of them knew the end was coming but very few would admit it. Some of the other prisoners were complaining about various things but I told them how damned lucky they were, here, rather than in some of the places they could be.

After a few days of regrouping we started the next part of our journey. About 50 of us started walking further into Germany. For the first couple of days, it wasn't bad. It is surprising what a little food will do. However, in the main cities it was very bad for the POWs in uniform. The people knew they were all fly-ers and they called them, "terror Fliegers." They had a lot of bad names hissed at them in anger and the Germans would throw things at them. I guess you couldn't blame them, as the Allies had been bomb-ing them night and day, trying to demoralise the people and bring the war to an end. Particularly dur-ing the last few months, the civilians didn't get much relief, as the Americans bombed in the daylight and the British and Allies at night. A few years previous the English had been bombed day and night, then it had been their turn, but the British hadn't started this war.

I was very scruffy looking in my old clothes and wooden shoes. I hung around at the back of the lines and the civilians just thought I was a Dutch prisoner. The guys at the front of the line were the "terror fliegers." I never got hit at all. Looking like a Dutch-man, I was often given food and things which the oth-ers weren't. I took full advantage of it. I sure laughed at the other guys. They were all very new at this and thought that things were very bad. They were nervous but they hadn't met the SS and the Gestapo. In com-parison, this was sort of like a boy scout hike to me.

There was no such thing as a bathroom. We would stop in a city square, or a similar area, and we would just have to relieve ourselves, wherever we were. Our guards liked to make public spectacles of us, but there was no way we were going to go in our pants. The German soldiers were never shy and would urinate any place. It is the other job that was more embarrassing.

The Germans did not expect us to try to escape anymore as we were getting deeper and deeper into Germany. There was very little food in Germany and we had to depend on the guards for the little bit we got. The guards protected us from the people as much as guarding us. Nobody told us where we were going or why, but it didn't really matter to us. We were only putting in time until the Allied forces caught up with us or the war came to an end.

About a week after we arrived at another dispersal camp which was the first organised camp I had been in. The others were all sort of make-shift type of places. This camp had prisoners from all over but, best of all, it had some Red Cross personnel in it. I got my first shower and a change of clothes; it had been over three months since I had taken my clothes of. The fellows I was with were relieved that I finally was able to take a shower. Now, we were on equal footing, all smelling clean and we could get dirty together now. I found it was quite a shock to the body, to have one's first shower. In fact, I could only take a little at a time as they didn't want me to pass out.

The change of clothes felt really great. I got a pair of boots with socks and was glad to get rid of the wooden shoes. However, they had served me well and I should have saved them for souvenirs. We were all given a blanket and a Red Cross parcel. The Red

Cross Organisation that provided the parcels was a God-send. I don't know what the POWs would have done without them. The parcels contained a can of Klim, which was powdered milk. The Klim can was about five inches high and five inches round and we would put a handle on the empty can, to use it as a cup or a cooking pot to boil things in. Many things were made out of Klim cans. There was also a can of Spam, the canned pork that everyone in the services knew about. It had replaced the corned beef of the First World War. After the war, some people had saved a special can of Spam for when we came home, but by then it was the last thing we wanted to see. The parcels also had a couple of cartons of American cigarettes, which were the main thing we used for trading. The guys that did not smoke had a great advantage. You could trade cigarettes for almost anything and they had the highest value. There were also a few chocolate bars and a few vitamin pills in the parcels as well as K rations, which were US army dinners. The parcels differed a little, so there was always a little excitement when getting one.

I talked to a Red Cross worker, who tried to get a letter to my wife and mother. I had been away for ten months now and had no contact with anybody. I tried to let them know I was OK. I guess the Red Cross did send one message but it got lost in the shuffle. It was very hard to get anything out of Germany as things were in disarray.

The respite didn't last long and we were off again very shortly. I had to pack this time. I had my blanket and part of a Red Cross parcel. We used to say, "God

Bless the Red Cross." This wasn't said in the religious way, it was just a saying. I never saw the Germans interfere with the Red Cross parcels or with their work. I'm not saying they never took from the Red Cross, I am saying, "I never saw them doing it." The Red Cross was a world peace organisation that didn't take sides, and worked according to the Geneva Convention.

There was a group of about fifty of us, all air crew. They marched us most of the day. As usual, we did not have a clue where we were going, but we knew we were not coming back here. We came to a big railway marshalling yard were all the box cars were held. W e didn't like being in these places as they were one of the Allies favourite bombing targets. Rail was the main way the Germans moved military materials to the front. We were put in a box car. On the side there was a sign, "Hommes 40 or 8 Chevaux", forty men or eight horses.

This, we found out was going to be our home for the next while. The big door was locked when we were travelling with the guards in another part of the train. Often, when we stopped, they would open the door and a German soldier would stand guard. There were a couple of square holes in the wall, up high, they were about six inches by ten inches. We could look out if we stood on our toes. That was our fresh air. W e would take turns looking out and tell the others what was happening.

We heard we were going south to a camp in southern Germany. We were actually being used as pawns constantly moving us away from the front lines. We had markings on top of our boxcars, "POW" and they would then put us in the middle of a freight train. This wasn't right, because according to the Geneva Convention, they weren't suppose to put POWs near a target of any kind. The high level bombers couldn't see the sign and the low level bombers didn't believe it.

We were a low priority. At the least excuse, we would be put on a siding and left there until we could be hooked onto another train that was going our way. I often wondered if there was anyone looking after the trains, and where they were going. It was very slow going but it didn't make much difference as we didn't know where we were going anyway. With all our bodies in the box car we weren't cold.

When we were on a siding in a marshalling yard, we would very often be next to a box car full of Jewish people. It was horrible we had fifty or sixty of us in our box car and we could all sit down. However, they had more than hundred and had to stand all the time. They were dressed in clothing that looked like striped pyjamas. They were so thin and gaunt looking. I was in bad shape, but they were much, much worse. We saw many that did not even have water to drink. If one died, they would just push the body out of the box car. They had no other choice. I don't think the guards ever opened their doors for fresh air or anything else. They included men, women and kids, all piled in packed in worse than animals. It must have been stifling in there, as they only had the small holes in the wall like ours. No one can tell me the Holocaust never happened. The little I saw of it was far worse than anything I ever saw on film after the war.

One day we were sitting in a siding, when we heard the bombers coming. The big door was opened and the guard was sitting at the door. We just knew they were going to bomb. It was a squadron of US Flying Fortresses. You could always tell when it was them as they glistened in the sky. They were all lining up on the bombing run, ready to drop their bombs. We jumped over the guard and out the door and ran and ran. Sometimes you think you can only run so far, but you can run a lot farther when you have to. The guard shot at us, but I think he shot in the air, as no one was hit. He had to put on a show! I guess he was frightened too, or maybe he was running as well. What a horrible whistle the bombs make when they are coming down! They sure bombed the hell out of the rail yard. We all agreed we would rather be up there dropping them, than be down below catching them. It seemed to last a long time, and that was the closest I had been to the bottom end of a big bombing raid.

When we were sure it was over we went back to the box car. The guard was there waiting for us. He was angry because he had been knocked out of the box car when we all clambered over him. He was also angry because our own planes dropped bombs on us, but our box car was not hit. The poor Jewish people were locked in their box car the whole time and it must have been horrible! We were frightened but it gave us a lot of exercise and something to talk about. Now I knew how the people must have felt being bombed day after day. No wonder they called us "terror fliegers". London and all of southern England had had it for years, during the first part of the war, night after night. Then later the Germans began sending over Buzz Bombs or Doodlebugs and the V2 rockets. They were scary and dangerous for the people they hit. They did quite a lot of damage, mostly to houses although some odd factories.

Our food arrived irregularly; nothing seemed organised. We only got our watery soup and bread when we happened to be in the right place at the right time. We only travelled a few miles a day and then we were parked on a siding again. There were a lot of trains, going back and forth to the front. The only priority we had was when they wanted to use our box car, to be in the middle of their train, so the aircraft would not bomb.

Finally, we stopped in a big marshalling yard outside a big city, where we were taken out of the box car and walked for a few hours. We soon came to the biggest camp I had ever seen. I think there were thousands of POWs in all many different sub-camps. We were put in a barrack here.

We scrounged around and found a thin straw mat each, and registered for our Red Cross parcel. W e soon learned what we were supposed to do and not do regarding all the rules and regulations. This was the Nuremburg POW Camp. I hoped it was going to be my home until the end of the war. I had travelled enough on their railway and I didn't need any more hiking.

Fig.8a POW's tried to make many things

Fig.8b German Cheese

Fig. 8c An Airmen on Squadron to an old Kriegie

Fig. 8d An old Kriegie meeting his nephew

Fig.8e An old Kriegie

Chapter Nine

Nuremburg to the Big March

The Nuremburg camp didn't have bunks or beds, but it was a lot better than the boxcars I had been in and a hell of a lot better than the three months when first captured that I had spent on cement floors. After sleeping on cold concrete floors, the wooden floor with a thin straw mat didn't feel that bad. There were a hundred of us in one hut, just room enough to lay down. The smell was horrible with that many men in such close quarters and no hot baths or soap. There was a lot of complaining and bitching and I'd tried to tell the fellows how tough things could really get. W e knew the end was in sight as we could hear the big guns in the distance.

We had roll call every morning as we all had to b e accounted for. It was called "Appel". Our senior officer had to get us all lined up for it. The dress was a mixture of Air Force uniforms, civilian clothes or whatever you had. A more scruffy bunch I had never seen. The German NCO's would be yelling but finally everything would quiet down and the counting would begin. The odd time someone would be missing or they counted wrong. This got the Germans very excited and the count would start all over again. They would always leave us standing there until they finished. It was here that we got our little propaganda speech, especially after a bombing. One day the Red Cross truck came, but it was almost full of clothes brushes. You can imagine how those went over. They just sat in a pile. There were a few tooth brushes. Now they were in heavy demand so each camp got a quota to be raffled off. It was a big exciting raffle but I didn't get one. A tooth brush would have really been great! Try going a few days without cleaning your teeth, (I had gone months) and you realise how important they are.

Our toilets, or latrines as we called them in England, were holes dug in the ground, about six feet deep, about four feet wide and twenty feet long. There were a couple of long poles on each side and that was where you sat. It was generally quite busy as a lot of the guys had dysentery, which is not very nice at the best of times.

In the morning we were given a cup of ersatz coffee and a piece of black bread. Later a horse-drawn cart would come into the camp and head for the kitchen, delivering a small hunk of meat and a sack of some kind of vegetables. It would be cooked up in a soup and that would be our supper. I can remember once looking at a piece of rotten potato and saying, "Look it's rotten," and carried on eating it. If we ever got a piece of meat, we would really chew it slowly, or save it until we went to bed, to give us something to really savour. I must admit by this time the Germans didn't have much to eat themselves.

We also got our Red Cross parcels, one every two weeks between two people. They were just great, and it was always very exciting because of what might be in them. One of the items I enjoyed most was de-lousing powder. Earlier on, when a Red Cross truck came with newspapers, I liked to take my time when visiting the latrine and read a newspaper, but those days were long gone. The smell was always bad. This pit was also used for other purposes. If anyone was caught stealing food from any one else or the kitchen they were thrown in the pit (that was a big deep hole in the ground with a couple of poles across which was our toilet.) They had a hell of a time getting out, and as we had no hot showers, everyone knew who they were for a long time. There was nothing lower then stealing food, as it was very scarce and everyone was hungry and was in the same boat.

We had absolutely no eating utensils at all. Some of the older POWs, who had been prisoners for a few years, had these things but we knew ones didn't. I made a wooden spoon first. I got a piece of wood and started going to work on it using a piece of glass as a knife. It took a long time but I had lots of this as I wasn't going anywhere. It worked pretty well, but rubbing your tongue on a piece of dry wood is really awful. It sort of goes right through you. I later found a small lid that had come off something from a Red Cross parcel, (there was nothing ever wasted from Red Cross Parcels). As I said, time didn't go fast but I liked to keep busy. Some of the fellows just sat around feeling sorry for themselves all day long, but I would try to find something to do. Firstly I pounded the centre with a stone and then I found a piece of wire to make a lip around the spoon. Secondly, I attached the wire and looped it around for a handle. This was deluxe utensil compared to my wooden spoon.

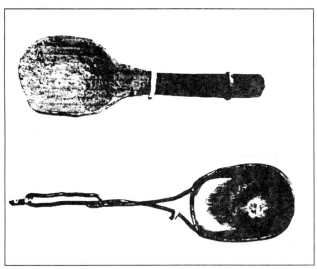

Fig.9a The Wooden spoon I made first and then I made the deluxe Metal Spoon

One night, around midnight, all hell broke loose. The camp was on a hill a couple of miles out from the city of Nuremburg and we could hear aircraft coming over. First, we saw the Pathfinders dropping their markers on the City. Then the main bomber stream started arriving, hundreds of them. We heard the roar of the planes, then the whine of the bombs coming down. We could hear the German anti-aircraft guns booming away. Then the bombs started going off. We all knew that, for many reasons, a few missed their target. We all wondered if the crews had been told in their briefing that we were down here, so close to the city. The huts literally bounced up and down. It looked like Halloween but this was April. I found out after the war, that there was 129 Halifax Bombers of No 4 Group and 14 Lancaster pathfinders on the Raid on Railway Yards. It was reported, that "the bombing attack was a great accuracy and they had lost no planes."

The Germans were yelling at anyone who left the huts or opened any black-out curtain. I was lucky because I had a good window seat. However, the guards were not very nice the next day. We assumed that quite a few people had been killed and maybe even some of the guards' immediate families. The city was almost destroyed. We knew the Allies must be getting close, but again, the German morale remained very high. We knew it was almost over, so why didn't they see that the end was so close? Maybe they did but were afraid to admit it, or didn't even know how to admit it.

There was a very high fence all around the compound with barbed wire on top. We couldn't go near it. There was another short electric fence about 10 feet inside the big one. We weren't even allowed past this short fence. We were all well warned that would be dead if we went into this area. The guards had machine guns pointing along the space between the fences. At night they had very bright lights along the fence, plus special spot-lights from the guard towers. The only chance of escape was if you built a tunnel. A lot of tunnels were built but only a few were successful. I did not see any organised escape because it was getting too close to the end of the war. The Great Escape was a big success. There is a very good book on this and they also made a movie of it. That escape was very well organised and well planned. They built a tunnel all the way out of the camp, and supplied forged identity papers and civilians clothes.

Fig.9b One way to escape. Some made it.

However, there weren't too many prisoners who actually got out of Germany. A large percentage were caught. Hitler was very annoyed and gave the order to have most of them shot. That was definitely against the Geneva Convention because it was our duty to try to escape and keep as many Germans as busy as possible. If they were doing that, they couldn't be fighting in the front lines.

Chapter Ten

The Big March to Mooseburg

April 1ST, April Fool's Day. First thing in the morning we started to hear a rumour that we would be moving out the next day. It came as a big surprise to all of us. We thought it was an April Fool's joke, but as the day went on we found out it wasn't a joke. W e were to be packed up, ready to leave by first thing in the morning. We had to make something to carry our blanket, Red Cross parcel and whatever else we might want to take. Some of the guys had accumulated quite a few things, but I had very little as I had not been in the camp that long.

First thing in the morning of April 2 we started off. There were quite a few camps and something like a thousand in each camp. I'm sure there were ten thousand of us. Now can you imagine this? We were all stretched out along the road, making a very long line. We were more or less told not to escape as the war was coming to an end. Food was getting very scarce and if we kept together we would have the Red Cross parcels as long as they lasted. The line of prisoners was miles long. Sometimes they would slow up at the front of the line for some reason or other and by the time it reached us, we would come to a stop. We wouldn't know if we were stopping for a rest, eat, sleep, or just slowing down.

When we stopped for the night, we would have to find someplace to sleep. Generally we slept in the forest at the side of the road. Some fellow prisoners would build a fire to keep warm or to cook and I can hear the yelling even now, "Put that fire out!" They were afraid of attracting aircraft that might start bombing us.

Before I left on this march, I had made a little burner which was great to cook small things on and it didn't make much of a glow. It was also very fast so if we only stopped for a short time, I could heat up something very quickly. I made it out of a Klim milk can. I had a little square box coming out of the side with a little fan in it. With some dry twigs and sticks it would get going very fast. It was like a miniature forge that blacksmiths used. Some of my fellow prisoners never even knew how to find dry wood. I would dig it out of the bottom of a tree or find some in the bottom of an old log. I was always picking up little chips or bits of wood on the road and kept them in my pocket. I was often referred to as the "crazy boy scout", but I survived better than a lot of them. There were many who just kept moping around, feeling sorry for themselves. In fact I tried to think of the whole march as kind of like a scout hike.

I think one of the worst things a fellow could get was dysentery. They would have to stop and go to the toilet very often. Then they would have to catch up with the column as weak as they were and getting weaker all the time. Often they would just have to give up and stay behind. The only thing we heard that would do any good for dysentery was to eat charcoal, so I ate lots of it. Good or bad, I don't know but I never got the trots! There was a lot of dysentery around. I guess it was the food we were eating, or not eating but I was very lucky and never got sick.

I was always on the lookout for things like dandelion leaves, so I could boil them up for greens. My father used to do this. One time I had gathered a lot of them but I didn't have time to cook them. My Red Cross buddy (we all had to have a buddy to share the Red Cross parcel with) was, for some reason, carrying them. I lost track of him for a couple of days. The first thing I asked him after been reunited was, "where are my dandelions?" He said, "I threw them away, I didn't know what to do with them!" I had the real urge to murder him. He was a real, useless tit. I should have given up on him.

One day I scrounged an egg. Now when you have not had an egg for a long time you really treasure it. I was looking forward to a nice, soft boiled egg. He decided to help me because I did most of the cooking, so he was going to cook my egg. Good God he hard boiled it! What a disappointment! I had been looking forward to it for days. He couldn't see anything wrong with what he did! The urge to kill again...

The German farmers were very good to us. They would come out to the road with big buckets of milk and give us each a cup full. The guards would get angry and chase them away. They would then go back to the end of the line and start giving it out again. I was very bitter towards the German SS and the Gestapo, but I had no bad feelings for the Wermacht (that is, the ordinary soldier), the farmers and other civilians.

We received almost no food from the German guards, because they didn't have any food themselves. We would barter food from farmers and people in small towns, using cigarettes to barter with. Soap was also very good. We prized everything in those Red Cross parcels. More over sometimes we would steal food out of the farm yards or anywhere we found it. When you are hungry, you do a lot of things you wouldn't normally do.

One day we stopped for a couple of hours for some unknown reason. I saw a big mill that was run by water power. The farmer had used it to grind wheat into flour. I swept up wheat from all around the place, in the corners etc. I brushed it clean and put it in the big hopper. Then I climbed up on the big wheel and rode it down. It took me a while but I wasn't in a hurry, although I had to be very quiet, as it was close to the farm house. I eventually made some flour. I took it back to where we were camping and decided to make some pancakes. I added powered milk and other odds and ends saved, including a couple of vitamin pills as I figured they would work like baking powder. They turned out very good. Now you have to remember we were on the hungry side and had not had pancakes for a long time, so the pancakes may not have been quite as good as I thought they were at the time.

One horrible thing that happened to us as we walked along were the American fighter bombers.

They loved to shoot at anything that moved. They would see us all on the road and would take it for granted that we were German soldiers on the move. It was horrible to have them come down and machine gun us all. They were shooting with 9mm guns or 20mm cannons which made a hell of a bang. It was a horrible feeling! To see the planes fly over was fine, but then when you heard them starting to dive, you knew they were coming after you. I always tried to keep a ditch in view, it gave me a little comfort. If those big guns hit a two foot tree they would knock it all to hell. We would get behind a tiny six inch tree and think we were safe. When I was young, I had read stories about how the ostrich would put his head in a hole. One day, when we were bombed by those fighter bombers, four prisoners were killed and four wounded. That was horrible! Some of these fellows had been prisoners from a few months to a few years. To get killed so close to the end of the war, and by our own fighters! Another group were hit a lot harder. There were twenty or so killed or injured. One day, we quickly wrote a big sign "POW" on the field using toilet paper, but it didn't help. They ignored it or didn't believe it.

We were almost bombed by a Kittyhawk squad-ron one day. They had the big hawk painted with very bright colours on the nose of the plane. They came right down and took a look at us. They were a squad-ron made up of black pilots (Tuskeegee Squadron). We could see them with a big grin on their faces. They dipped their wings and flew off. We were not bombed after that, so I guess they reported back that we were POWs on the move.

The Red Cross seemed to be well organised. Every two weeks, wherever we were, they found us. W e would see their big white trucks with the big red crosses on them. As I said we were all in pairs and got one parcel between us, every two weeks. The American parcels were my favourite as they had US cigarettes in them and more of them. English cigarettes weren't as good, less popular, and we got a fewer of them.

Coming into the middle of April , we enjoyed some very nice days. Spring was on its way and as usually was a beautiful time of the year. With the weather so nice and the summer seemed nice to look forward to. During some of those nice Spring days one could almost forget the war.

Fig.10a Roll Call or in German "Appel"

In sixteen days we only received a bowl of soup, a couple of pounds of potatoes and 1-1/2 loaves of bread from the Germans. So it was either scrounge food, barter for it, or depend on the Red Cross. The Germans didn't have food supplies anymore and the guards themselves didn't have much food at all, and they didn't have the Red Cross parcels.

After sixteen days, during which we walked 120 kilometres, we came to a very large prison camp, much bigger than any I had seen so far. It was called Mooseburg #7A POW camp. Again, I figured this was to be my last stop.

Delousing Powder from the Red Cross (Great Stuff)

Paper bandage the Germans used

Part of the wooden soles for shoes used by Germans at that time

Fig.10b German soles for shoes and paper bandage plus our delousing powder

Chapter Eleven

Mooseburg to England

We were scattered through out a lot of very crowded bunkhouses. Some of the prisoners in the camp had been there for a long time. There was a mixture of American, Canadian, British, in fact prisoners from all of the Allied forces, including the army, air force and navy. There was also a very large camp of Russian prisoners next door.

There were a hundred of us in each hut. The bunks were very large and would accommodate two people wide, two people in length and were in three tiers. That meant twelve people slept in each section. They were very wobbly, being made out of wood and built three high, but also because people had taken some of the cross braces off to burn in the stove for heat or cooking.

The Russians were in a camp next door to us. Their living conditions were very sad and they only had sacks and rags for clothes. They were very thin, weak and gaunt looking, just like the Jewish people in the concentration camps. The war between the Russians and Germans was very different to the war between the Western Allies and the Germans with the big difference being that they didn't observe the Geneva Convention. We weren't doing too badly compared to them. The Germans treated the Russians horribly and vice versa, the Russians treated their German prisoners just as badly. When the Germans advanced east across Russia, they plundered, raped and murdered millions of Russians. So when the Russians came back west, they did the same thing to the Germans.

The end of the war was now getting nearer. We could hear the heavy guns as they were very close. The day before General Patton arrived, the Germans gave the camp up and turned it over to the senior officers of the POWs. Those officers had to keep some kind of order, as the war wasn't over yet and there were still lots of SS around who were not giving up to the very end.

On April 28th, General Patton and his soldiers came in the front gate. What a great feeling to be free at last ! I'll never forget an American soldier throwing me a loaf of white bread. I was sure it was angel food cake. It was delicious after a diet of black German sour dough bread.

The Germans all left and the camp, it was then organised by the senior allied officers in the camp. There had to be some sort of organisation in the camp to give out our Red Cross parcels and to keep things in order generally the American Army didn't want us running all over the place, as they had a war to finish. There was still another week or so of tough fighting. It wasn't a big problem to get wood to cook with now, we just broke pieces off the huts. We didn't care what they looked like, as we had no intention of being there long, we were all going home.

I headed out one day, with a group of Russians, looking for food. There was a pig farm close by and we started to chase this pig. We ran and we ran until the pig dropped. My Russian companions started cutting it up and I was right in there with them, but, firstly I couldn't speak Russian and secondly there were a lot of them, so I only got the head and neck. I wasn't complaining, as there was still a lot of eating in the neck and head.

I was cooking for a couple of other guys who spent most of their time moping around. We had roast pork, that is, pork cooked on the end of a stick on a open fire, fried pork, sort of done in a pan and boiled pork. I also found a chicken pen, but unfortunately, I was too late to get any of them. However, I kept looking and eventually found a couple of eggs, and a few vegetables, carrots and beets, that were really great. We had powdered skim milk in our Red Cross parcels and I was told, that it would whip if one worked long enough. I beat it in a can with my spoon for about an hour, and although it never really whipped, with a little imagination it tasted good. One day when I was out looking for food, I came across a group of Americans soldier who gave me a gallon of corned beef hash. I sat down and started to eat it. I ate and ate until I was sick, but what a wonderful feeling to be really full and still have food left over!

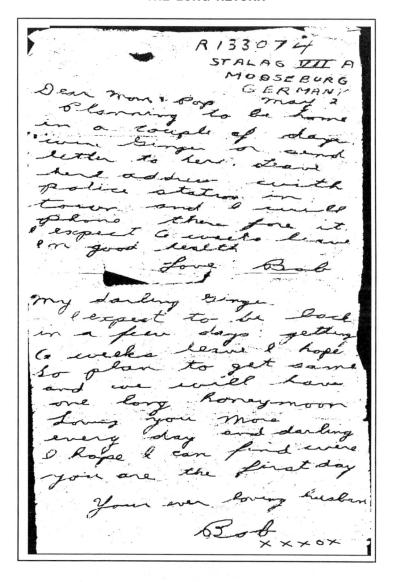

Fig.11a A letter written May 2nd on toilet paper. I wrote Ginger and her Mom. They received this letter weeks after my return

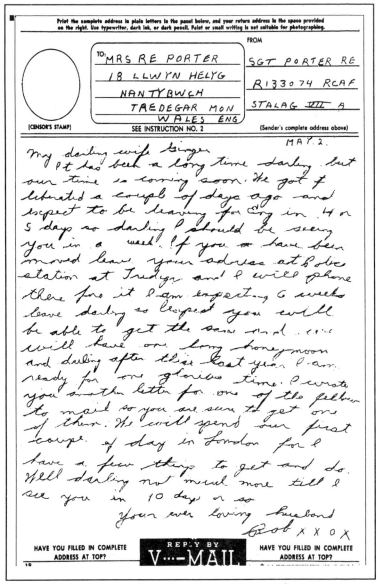

Print the complete address in plain letters in the panel below, and your return address in the space provided on the right. Use typewriter, dark ink, or dark pencil. Faint or small writing is not suitable for photographing.

FROM

TO: MRS RE PORTER
18 LLWYN HELYG
NANTYBWCH
TREDEGAR MON
WALES ENG

(CENSOR'S STAMP)
SEE INSTRUCTION NO. 2

SGT PORTER RE
R133074 RCAF
STALAG VIII A

(Sender's complete address above)

MAY. 2.

My darling wife Ginger
It has been a long time darling but
our time is coming soon. We got +
liberated a couple of days ago and
expect to be leaving for Eng in 4 or
5 days so darling I should be seeing
you in a week. If you or have been
moved leave your adress at Police
station at Tredigr and I will phone
there for it I am expecting 6 weeks
leave darling so Iexpect you will
be able to get the same and we
will have one long honeymoon
and darling after this last year I am
ready for one glorious time. I wrote
you another letter for one of the fellows
to mail so you are sure to get one
of them. We will spend our first
coupe. of day in London for I
have a few things to get and do.
Well darling no more till I
see you in 10 days or so
Your ever loving husband
Bob X X O X

HAVE YOU FILLED IN COMPLETE
ADDRESS AT TOP?

REPLY BY
V---MAIL

HAVE YOU FILLED IN COMPLETE
ADDRESS AT TOP?

Fig. 11b Another letter I wrote to Ginger, May 2 1945 through the Red Cross "V Mail." We received it a month after coming home

AIR MINISTRY,

73-77, Oxford Street, London, W.I.

7th May 1945.

CAN/ Re 133074/P.4/CAS/C.4.

Dear Mrs. Porter,

Further to my letter of the 21st December, 1944, I wish to inform you that further information has been received concerning your husband, Flight Sergeant Robert Edward Porter, but which, unfortunately, does not establish whether he is now alive.

A report has been received to the effect that your husband was with a party of Allied servicemen who were making their way back to Allied territory on the night of the 2nd /3rd January 1945. The party was subjected to considerable fire by the Germans; at this point the party was separated and your husband and others were last seen running across the ice in a badly flooded area.

A further report has reached us which states that two members of the party were killed. No further information has been received concerning your husband, and in view of the lapse of time, grave consideration must be given to the possibility that he may have lost his life at that time.

You may be assured that immediately upon receipt of further news, you will be informed.

Please accept my deepest sympathy with you during this trying time.

Yours sincerely,

E J Figg F/L

for (J S. Harris),Wing Commander for Air
Officer Commanding in chief,
R.C.A.F. Overseas.

Mrs. R.E. Porter
18, Lewyn Helyg
Nantybwch
Tredegar, Mon

Fig.11c May 7th. (A copy of a Letter) my wife received, grave consideration that I may have lost my life. Has been re-typed for clarity

ROYAL CANADIAN AIR FORCE

OTTAWA, Canada, 10th May, 1945.

BOMBER MAIL

FILE NO: R.133074 (R.O. 4)

Canadian Casualty Branch,
Air Ministry,
P.4 Cas (Can),
73-77 Oxford Street,
LONDON, W.1, England.

CAN/R133074 Flight Sergeant PORTER, R.E.

1.   It is requested, please, that no steps
whatever be taken to initiate Presumption of Death action
on Flight Sergeant Porter, without these Headquarters being
first advised of your intention to take such action.

(T.K. McDougall),
Group Captain,
for Chief of the Air, Staff.

Fig.11d Letter from RCAF to Canadian Casualty Branch. No steps to be taken on presumption of my death

"THE LONG RETURN"

ADDRESS REPLY TO:

THE SECRETARY.
DEPARTMENT OF NATIONAL DEFENCE FOR AIR.
OTTAWA, ONTARIO.

OUR FILE R.133074 (R.O. 4)
REF. YOUR
DATED

ROYAL CANADIAN AIR FORCE

<u>AIR MAIL</u>

OTTAWA, Canada, 10th May, 1945.

Mr. C.A. Porter,
3406 Imperial Street,
New Westminster, B.C.

Dear Mr. Porter:

Further to our letter of March 16th, a report has now been received which, although containing nothing definite concerning the present whereabouts or fate of your son most unfortunately indicates that he may have lost his life.

This report states that your son was one of a party of thirteen allied service men who were evading and were making their way back to liberated territory in Holland on the night of January 2nd. The party was subjected to considerable fire by the Germans and they were forced to separate. While some took cover, your son and some of the others moved off, and it is reported that your son was shot when they attempted to escape across the ice in a badly-flooded area, while under fire from three German machine gun posts. Your son was dressed in civilian clothes at that time but was wearing his identification disc. He and the others with him were not seen again.

The above information was obtained from members of the party who took cover and did not attempt to cross the ice. You will understand, of course, that there is no official confirmation that your son was shot. However, two other Royal Canadian Air Force personnel who were believed to be with your son when the attempt was made to cross the ice, have now been reported by the Germans through the International Red Cross at Geneva to have lost their lives. As no further information has been received concerning your son, and in view of the above report and the time which has elapsed, it unhappily appears that he also may have lost his life on the night of January 2nd.

--- 2 ---

R.C.A.F. G. 32B
50031-1 44 (3778)
11.Q. 885-G-32B

Fig.11e Page 1 of 2 pages May 10th letter to my Mother from RCAF, the Day before Mother's Day. A very sad letter

--- 2 ---

Pending confirmation of the above report, Air Ministry advises that your son is still being considered as "missing".

I wish to assure you that no effort will be spared in an endeavour to locate the whereabouts of your son or ascertain his fate. There is a Royal Air Force and Dominion Air Force Missing Research and Enquiry Service now in operation in Europe whose function it is to obtain as complete information as possible on all personnel believed to be casualties in territories which were occupied by the Germans and are now liberated and on whom full particulars have not yet been received. It is hoped that through this Service additional information will be obtained. Please be sure that immediately any further news is received it will be communicated to you at once.

I very deeply regret to have to pass on to you a report with information of such a nature, especially when it is still indefinite, but felt sure that you would wish to have any information received by this Department concerning your son.

I trust that the knowledge that your son, together with others of his high calibre, was willing to offer his life as his contribution to ensure a lasting peace which we hope the Allied Victory in Europe will result in, will give you courage and sustain you during this period of uncertainty and sorrow.

May I offer you my most sincere sympathy at this time of anxious waiting.

Yours sincerely,

R.C.A.F. Casualty Officer,
for Chief of the Air Staff.

Fig.11f Page 2 of 2 May 10th letter to my mother the day before Mothers' Day

They started transporting us back to England, but it was a very big job with approximately 40,000 of us to move. We were sorted into our different camps and they decided to have a big raffle to see who got out first, second, and third. A large camp of East Indians won and were the first to leave. I was in the fourth or fifth bunch to leave. We were very lucky to have been liberated by the US army. The POWs who were liberated by the Russians didn't have it nearly as good. The only change that occurred when the Russians liberated a camp was that German guards were exchanged with Russian guards. Further more, the Russians weren't going to liberate Allied prisoners until the Russians prisoners were sent back to Russia. The big problem was that all our prisoners wanted to go home while the Russians didn't want to go back to Russia. Russian POWs weren't treated very well when they got back home, where many ended up in Siberia, so they wanted to stay in the west. In the end, Allied prisoners had to escape from the Russians.

By May the 7th the war was pretty well over for us but it wasn't officially over until May 8th. On the night of May 7th we had a huge fire in the front of the camp. We burned everything we could get our hands on shutters from the windows, tables, beds, so-called mattresses made from straw, doors, wagons and anything we could carry.

On May the 8th it was our turn to head out. W e walked about 20 kilometres to an airfield called Regensberge. I never got on a plane that day, but met a crew who were taking guys back in Lancaster bombers. I asked them to radio down to Ginger when they were flying over Stratford-on-Avon OTU, that I was on my way home. They never did or they did, and no one passed the message on, as Ginger never got it. I had been away for almost a year now and still didn't know if anyone knew that I had survived or not. Before nightfall they told us we were not going to leave that day. I knew there was a small town, called Lanshot not far away, so I decided to see if I could find a comfortable place to sleep. The town was almost empty. I guess the people left when the fighting was going on. I found an apartment that was empty with a bed in it, and there I spent the night.

I flew out of Germany on May the 10th. What a great feeling to be heading for England! We didn't know where we were going. We thought we were going straight to England but we only got as far as Reims, in France where we landed near a very big US army camp. Immediately upon landing, we were made to form two line-ups lousy prisoners this way, non-lousy ones that way. A lot of us were lousy. They then used big hoses to blow de-lousing powder up your pant legs, down the front of your pants, and up your shirt. They were very thorough, but it was good! Then we had a full turkey dinner with all the trimmings, with fresh beans, and peaches for desert. It was great! Most of us had two helpings but really could not eat it all as our stomachs had shrunk. It was kind of nice, as the food was served by German POWs. I think they knew we were kind of temperamental as we were ex-POW and some of us weren't very nice to them.

Later that night we were in the air again, flying to England. We landed in a RAF station in southern England and I tried to phone Ginger. However, as it was war-time, I couldn't get the telephone number of the station she was at, and her parents didn't have a phone. I called the police in her town and left a message for her father that I would call back the next day. At the station they fed us bacon and eggs, all we wanted. They went all out for us. They called out over the intercom inviting the WAF's to come to the mess for a party with a bunch of POWs, and they wouldn't have to work the next day. We had a great party! It didn't take much beer to get us high. I can remember sitting in the middle of the floor, all my odds and ends spread out around me, with a big smile on my face. We were scattered all over the base to sleep, but I slept right in the mess. I wanted to be close to the kitchen, I wasn't dumb. Next day, we were off to Bournemouth, the RCAF'S main transfer centre, we were given a lunch, a train ticket, but no money and off we went again. I bummed a shilling off a stranger on the street to phone Ginger's father again. I told them I was an ex-POW and trying to get in touch with my wife. I phoned the police station again to see if my father-in-law was there. I never knew there were two Tredegars, which was the town she was from. This time I phoned Old Tredegar. The other time I had phoned New Tredegar, so I still hadn't found him. My money was gone and my train was coming, so off I went. The next time we stopped, I did it all over again and finally spoke to him. He had been running back and forth from one police station to the other.

He finally got hold of Ginger up at her station, to let her know I was alive, well, and back in England. This is when I found out that none of them had known that I was alive. In fact they were quite sure I was dead. It was a shock to all of them ! The first thing I did when I got to Bournemouth was to send a telegram to my mother to tell her I was safe.

The day before Mother's Day she had received a letter from Ottawa saying that they had given up hope; on Mother's Day she received my telegram saying that I had arrived safely in England. This was the first news they had heard from me in eleven months. The day after Mother's Day the RCAF phoned my mother to tell her to disregard the last letter. Then they sent her another telegram. I talked to Ginger on the phone and we started to make arrangements to get together. I was told I had to stay in Bournemouth for a week of interrogations of a sort. They wanted to know where I had been for the last year. They told me what had happened to my crew and where they were buried. I found out that Bill Gardiner was buried in an unmarked grave, as nobody could recognise his body and didn't know if it was him or me. The airforce then got in touch with his wife Dorothy, to let her know that it was his body and not mine. Very tough on his family, but very lucky for me and mine. I had a interview with a reporter from Vancouver who was writing for the "The Maple Leaf", an airforce paper.

Ginger came down to Bournemouth as soon as she could get away. They had known on the air- force station she was on, that I had been missing, so there was no problem with her getting leave. As soon as my week was up and after they had finished checking me over, including having been kept on a diet until my stomach got back in order, Ginger and I went up to London. I was very displeased with headquarters in London.

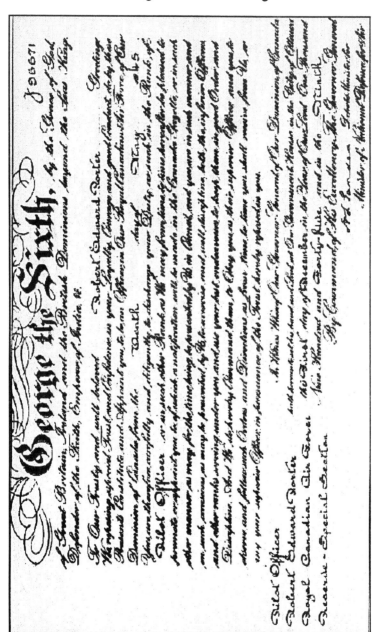

***Fig. 11 g I received my Commission dated May 10th
1945***

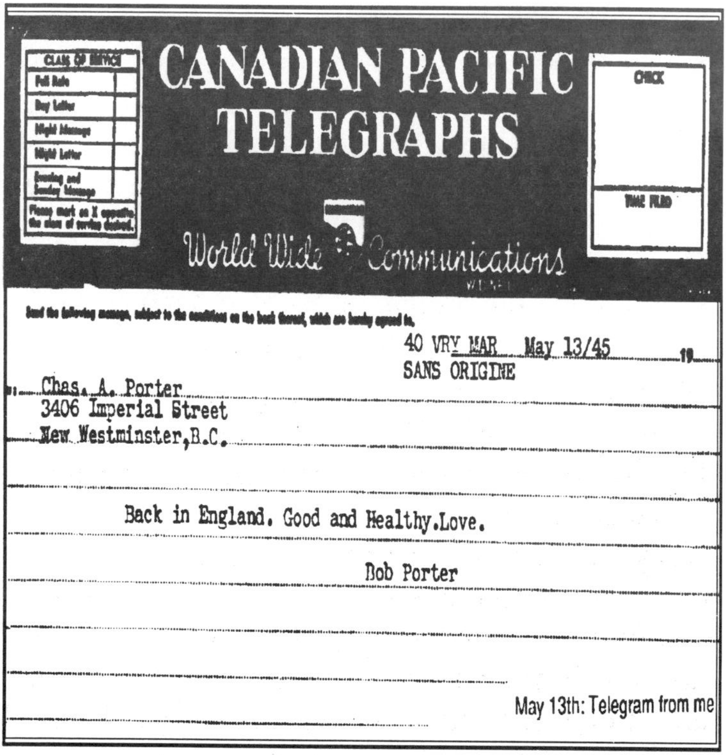

CANADIAN PACIFIC TELEGRAPHS

World Wide Communications

40 VRY MAR May 13/45 19

SANS ORIGINE

Chas. A. Porter
3406 Imperial Street
New Westminster, B.C.

Back in England. Good and Healthy. Love.

Bob Porter

May 13th: Telegram from me

Fig.11h Mother's Day morning, my mother received this telegram from me. The first she had heard from me in almost a year

Normally when someone was shot down they automatically got a commission or a raise in rank, but as no one knew where I was or whether I was still living, my file was just put on the shelf and left there. It wasn't only the rank but the pay that went with it that I had lost. They couldn't do anything in Bournemouth, because all of this was done in London. Consequently, I was very mad. I would not wear my hat or my rank on my shoulders. If service police stopped me, I just told them I was an ex-POW who had just gotten back and they wouldn't say anything. They had to be practical. What could they do to someone who had been a POW for a year? We had a lot of trouble getting a hotel room and had to go away from the centre of London, as all of the hotels were full. I found out later that most of them had been reserved for ex-POWs but no one told us that. I got Ginger settled in the hotel room. They were real snotty to us. A WAF with a Canadian shacking up and saying we were man and wife! We left our wedding picture on the dresser and went out for a while, knowing they would go into our room.

They were sure different when we got back. What a difference a little piece of paper such as a wedding certificate or a wedding picture makes. I headed down to headquarters. The buses were very cheap and it only cost me one tuppence to get there. The bus seemed to go straight to downtown London, no problem. When I arrived at headquarters, they didn't give me any problems. I was given my WO1 (warrant officer one) rank right away and papers put through for my commission, but they would not back date it to when I got shot down. They claimed it couldn't be back-dated that long, so I lost a year of back pay. They gave me a clothing allowance and some clothes' ration coupons to buy my new uniform as a WO1. I came out of head quarters feeling much better but maybe I came out a different door because everything looked different. I had in my mind to go straight up the main street but all the streets looked the same and none went straight. I had not written down the name of the hotel and I didn't have a clue where I should go. Back to square one! I took the name and address of the theatres, found a cab and told him my problem. So we started to drive from one theatre to another.

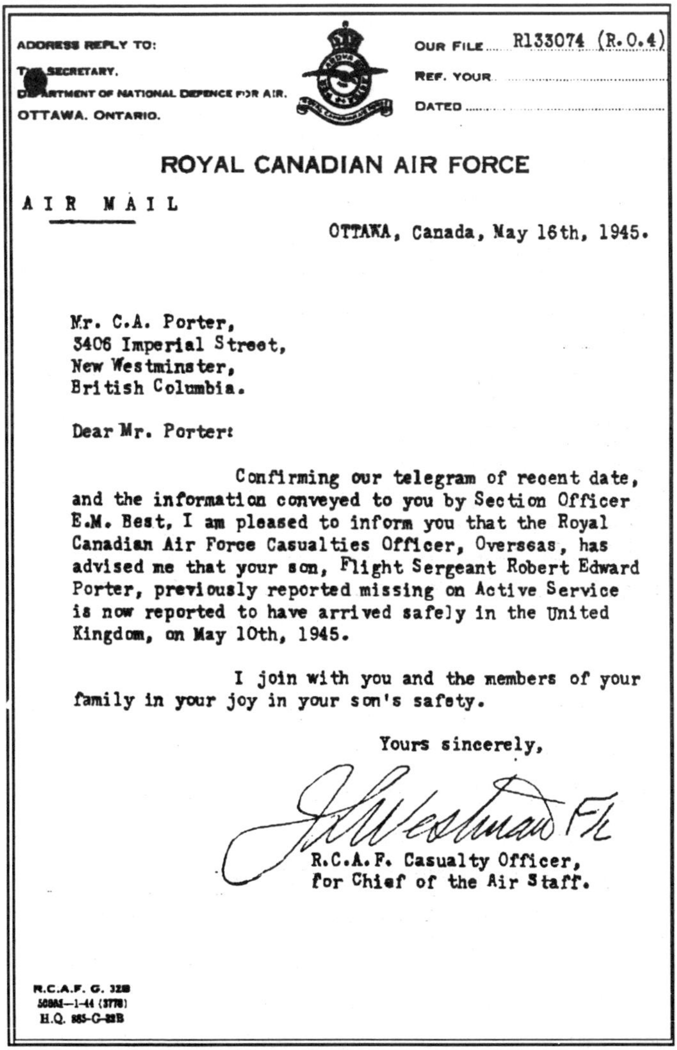

ADDRESS REPLY TO:
THE SECRETARY,
DEPARTMENT OF NATIONAL DEFENCE FOR AIR,
OTTAWA, ONTARIO.

OUR FILE R133074 (R.O.4)
REF. YOUR
DATED

ROYAL CANADIAN AIR FORCE

AIR MAIL

OTTAWA, Canada, May 16th, 1945.

Mr. C.A. Porter,
3406 Imperial Street,
New Westminster,
British Columbia.

Dear Mr. Porter:

Confirming our telegram of recent date, and the information conveyed to you by Section Officer E.M. Best, I am pleased to inform you that the Royal Canadian Air Force Casualties Officer, Overseas, has advised me that your son, Flight Sergeant Robert Edward Porter, previously reported missing on Active Service is now reported to have arrived safely in the United Kingdom, on May 10th, 1945.

I join with you and the members of your family in your joy in your son's safety.

Yours sincerely,

J.L. Westman F/L

R.C.A.F. Casualty Officer,
for Chief of the Air Staff.

R.C.A.F. G. 32B
50M—1-44 (3778)
H.Q. 885-G-32B

Fig.11i May 16th. Letter my mother received from the RCAF

THE MAPLE LEAF   Thursday, May 31, 1945

His Friends Thought He Was Gone For Good

Wife's Faith Rewarded as Airman Returns

BOURNEMOUTH Given up for dead by almost everyone but his young English bride, Fl Sgt. Robert Porter, Burnaby, B.C., bomb-aimer, arrived in England after more than seven month's evading capture and several months in German prison camps.

Porter was first reported missing in June of last year, after an attack against Cologne, and until his arrival in England no word of his where a bouts has been heard by his wife, parents or friends.

At the "R.C.A.F. Released Prisoner of War Centre" here he told how he kept out of the clutches of the Germans, posing as a Dutch civilian. "I was blow out over Holland after our bomber was blew up in mid-air," he said, "the rest of the crew did not make it"

"and I got in touch with a Dutch man, who agreed to help me. I rode on the back of his bicycle, to his house, past couple of German soldiers, neither of whom recognized my uniform."

After moving into three different homes, Porter said, he finally settled in one near Utrecht, which he calls his "permanent home in Holland." Here he was fitted out with civilians clothes.

The Vancouver airman had to leave the village at Christmas time, when the Gestapo started rounding up every Dutch man between the ages of 16 and 65 to work in Germany. He traveled through Holland to the Rhine, which he crossed by ferry after helping a German soldier push it off the river bank, but was finally captured after he and some friends were sighted by sentries.

"For four hours they chased us across the frozen, flooded country side. We made it to a hut and hid, but during the night there was a thaw and the melting ice around isolated us like an island, and we were captured."

Treated as a saboteur and terrorist, Robert was turned over to the German secret police and was threatened with shooting so often he finally didn't care. In March he was transferred to a prisoner of war camp and was liberated by American Army troops in May. "The 21-years-old airman reported that his telegram to his wife, who is serving in the W.A.A.F., was the first word that she had received about him since he had been reported missing."

She never lost hope, although most of my friends figured that I was "gone for good" he said.

Fig.11j Write up in the "The Maple Leaf" the Air force Paper

My luck wasn't too good, we didn't hit the right theatre until the third try. It cost me tuppence to get to headquarters and almost two pounds to get back to my hotel. Ginger and I saw a bunch of shows and did lots of talking, trying to catch up on what had happened in the last year. When I was in London, I wrote my mother a long letter As she had not heard from me for almost a year there was a lot to tell her. This was a nineteen page letter showing my feelings as they were then. I could not say much about my time in Holland as the war was not fully over. The return address was my wife's home in South Wales. This was a nineteen page letter, when I wrote it in long hand. After my mother had given it to everybody to read and sending it all over, it was almost totally worn out.

---

18 llwyn Helyg Nantybwch
Tredegar Mon. S. Wales
May 15,1945

Dear Mom,
   I wrote an airmail from this morning, but could not write very much, on it, as so much has happen in the last year. So, I hope, I will get to make this a long one and then telephone you.
   That night, we were going to the Ruhr. Which was really a hot target, we were chased by fighters, once going in and once going out of the target. We dropped our bombs and almost home safe and sound we could see the English channel on the Radar and that always looked good. But over Holland, there was a lot of flack around all the way back from the target. We must have been hit in the oxygen lines because our Aircraft was on fire in the fuselage. I was helping Gardy, the navigator with the Radar. I grabbed a fire extinguisher, and headed back to the fuselage. It had started too fast and grown to big, to put out. It was a mass of flames, by this time Bill our pilot could see it and new it was hopeless and told us to bail out. Our English Engineer opened the escape hatch and got it jammed. Before doing so, he took off his oxygen. So flying at 22,000 feet, he passed out. I tried to get down and get him out of the way, but while doing so, the gas tanks blew up. Last I remember, the fire was all around us. We were being thrown from one side of the aircraft, to the other. I more or less said my prayers then, said good-bye to Ginger, and you and that was all until I came conscious at about 7000 feet. I figured because, I wouldn't have got enough oxygen, until 10,000 feet. I had my parachute on, but it was not opened. So, I felt on my chest for my shoot and it was not there.
   That was scary, I felt a tug on my shoulder, my shoot had come unhooked and was above my head I had enough sense to reach up and pull the ripe cord and open it. I slowed down very quick. I could see our aircraft miles away, burning. I landed safely, in a tree; that was the last I saw of all my crew.
   I found out later that "Bill Smith", my pilot and "Sid Wilson" rear gunner, were killed and buried at Amersfort. I will never forgive the Engineer, for getting the escape hatch jammed which I figure, got those two killed, according to one

225

of your letters you had sent Ginger "Glen Taylor" my mid-upper gunner was killed. The other three, I know nothing about, except what Jack Friday wrote from a "P.O.W. camp, that I was not so lucky as he figured I was dead. I think, he must have seen one of my crew. I would sure love to meet them again. They were a swell bunch. I had a lot of my hair burned, my eyebrows, and my hands a little. A large bang on my arm, a couple on each leg and a knock on the knee, but I was feeling good enough to walk.

It was a terrible night, raining and blowing, which I guess, helped me get away from the vicinity of my parachute, and where I landed. Later the next day, I made friends in Holland and they really treated me swell.

They hid me, fed me, clothed me, gave cigars and all, I even had a tailor make me a suit for my birthday, a barber came around to the house. I had it good, and really swell. I will never forget the people I lived with in Holland. When one comes to think of all they did for me. And if they had of been caught by the Germans his wife and two kids, would have been shot.

I sent a couple of letters out, when I was in Holland. I was pretty sure, you would have known all about me. I guess, they never got all the way through. There's a lot that happened from June, until January 03, but it is best, I think, not to write it in here as the war is not yet over and may endanger someone life in Holland, but I will be able to tell you all about it, when I get back.

On January 02, we started our escape through the lines to freedom. It might have been best for me to have stayed in Holland, until the end, but seven months is a long time, to sit around and never know for sure if you knew I was there. The possibility of being posted as dead, after six months.

We had crossed, the German line with very little trouble and was going South near Opheusden and the Germans, opened fire on us. The country had been all flooded and frozen. Some of the ice, would hold us, some would not, the water was from one inch to two or three feet. We started our mad run and all got separated. I was there with a Army Sergeant Major Wilf Berry and a Captain Roger Schjelderup from near Vancouver. The Germans would shoot flares at us, then machine gun us. We were running in water, on ice, or breaking ice half swimming. Wherever we were when the flares came, we hit the ground or the water or the ice. I lost my shoes on the ice and I was bare footed all night. My feet were sure cold, but lucky not frozen, after four hours of running and being chased.

Wilf and I hid up in a little shack until daylight. I never in my life, spent such a cold night. Our clothes practically frozen on us. The Sergeant Major Wilf Berry, had a bullet in his arm. We were fed up and ready to give in at daylight. Very luckily I had some dry tobacco in a tin, in my inside pocket. I took the cotton batten out and to get a light. I had a couple of frozen apples and our moral was up 50%.

"THE LONG RETURN"

We were ready then, to keep fighting and try to get back. Then, we heard the British guns and rifles fire and we knew, they were close. In fact, about a kilometre away but we found we were on almost an island. As it had gotten warmer the ice melted, only one way off and we headed that way hoping it was to the English lines but it wasn't, it was in to the Germans lines. So we were taken prisoners, which was sure "hell" after waiting seven months to get back and get caught a kilometre away, that is bad luck. The Germans who captured us treated us pretty good but we were taken to jail near " Arnhem ", for interrogation.

We wore civilian clothes, and had a sten gun, with us. The Germans took a very dim view of this and we knew they could have legally shot us. We don't knew why, they never!

But we were taken to Dodewaard and then to Felp, and were under the German Army Secrete Police, they were not so nice and very rough. We were there for about three weeks, in solitaire on a cup of soup and piece a bread per day, plus a cup of German ersatz coffee. We were interrogated for hours at a time, day or night. They were trying to find out which Dutch people had hid us and helped us. If we had told a dozen or so we would have been shot and the links broken. We told nothing and said: they could shoot us. They used to get so damned mad at us.

I had written a letter to Ginger to be sent through you, a week before I left, and the Germans had got it. I had written on rice paper and then rolled it up very tight. We took a comb and drilled a hole in it and put the note in the comb. A courier going through the line was taking it and he must have got caught, God knows what happened to him. This letter saying: "I had lived with this Captain Roger Schjelderup" from Courtney also one of his letter to his Mother. I had always told the Germans I had lived alone in a barn and knew no one, he jumped up, called me a damn liar and kicked me out of the room, a couple of hours later, he called me back, asked me: "Was I ready to tell the truth?". I said: "yes". He asked a few questions, including; had I written a letter? and had I lived alone? I told him I wrote none and lived alone. He sat down with on sarcastic smile. Passed me the letter that I had written, asked me: "Did I know Roger Shelderopp". It was sure a blow because it blew all my story. He was tired, physically kicked me out of the office, and back to my cell, I had time to make up a new story including Roger.

Dutch men were being beaten in the next room. They never badly tortured us, but we were expecting it any day!

When I lost my shoes, the Germans would only give me an old pair of wooden clogs which I had to learn to walk with in a hurry. Then we were sent up to another prison in Utrecht: Which we again were put alone into a cell and gave a cup of coffee, for breakfast, a cup of watery soup for lunch and piece of bread for supper. The days were really long and we got so damned hungry. Just sitting there, day and night, no smoke, just thinking, after three weeks, we were sent to another concentration prison in Germany. We know all hopes of escape were gone, once we were out of Holland.

We only had one chance, but the lock jammed and we couldn't get it opened at the end. In the morning, the Germans tried to open the door and couldn't, so they knew, we had tried and put double locks, and a few more guards on us. This prison, in Germany, was worse, a cement cell, with cement floor and no heat. Our breath would condense on the ceiling and get about five or six large drops of water down a minute. We slept on the floor with no blanket. These were, all political prison, run by "SS." and "Gestapo". The way they treat the political prisoners is terrible and not propaganda. I have seen them, so I know.

The food here, was the same. I got very thin, every time I stood up, I had to hang on to something or I would pass out. Once they made me face the wall one afternoon and I passed out after about seven minutes of it. Smoking, we missed a lot. We would go so slow as to pick up a German cigarette butt, 1/2" long, was really a good one and five or six of us, smoke it. A person loses a lot of self respect and pride in times like that. I had a bath on December 23 and clean clothes. The Germans would not give us soap, towels or nothing to wash with. I was beginning to get high by this time.

It was March tenth, I got my bath and clean clothes. I literally stunk and that is not a word of a lie. When I wanted to go to sleep, I would put my nose down the front of my sweater. I just went off in a dream. (I am now having at least one bath a day) it sure is good. We were almost three weeks, in this first prison in Germany.

We then left for a collection type of camp, which thank God, was a P.O.W. camp and not a political prison camp which was "hell". We were then classed as "P.O.W. all the time before, we were always referred to as spies and terrorists. We knew we were safe, at least not talking about being shot, or beat up and no more solitary confinement. We got a few smokes there, and found the food much better. Instead of having one in a cell, we had seven or eight which I don't know which is worse. But treatment in general improved. Stayed here a week and got put with the Air force. I was sure sorry to loose the army types which I had been with.

We went up to "Muenster" where I stayed there one night and there wasn't a building standing in the whole place, not a wall, not a door, just a square mile or so of rubble. That is the German City of today, nothing left." Nuremberg, Frankfurt" and many others I saw were like that. The people were very bitter naturally. Our guards, then were not to keep us from escaping but keep the people away from us. We sure kept close to the guards. I never let them out of my sight.

We, then went to Frankfort by box car which was no fun because our aircraft were bombing and shooting the trains and rail-yards up all the time. I never got hit, but I know many of those that did.

"THE LONG RETURN"

At Frankfurt, I was interrogated again and left a couple of days later, for a place call " Wetslow " and to me, it was wonderful, that was about middle of March. I had my first wash, a real hot shower, got clean clothes, a tooth brush, a wonderful thing when you have not had one for 3 months. Also a Red Cross parcel, in a "P.O.W." camp a Red Cross box is a great luxury. The food in them was wonderful, especially to me, because two and a Half months of bread and soup soon loose their taste. We stayed here for a week, then started on our way to a permanent camp which was only about 3 or 4 hundred miles away, we travelled by box car, but it took us many weeks, to get there.

There, was maybe 50 of us, in a box car about 3/4 or 1/2 the size of ours at home. Just barely enough floor space for every one to sit down, and half stretch his legs out. We would go a little way and then stop, the railway would get bombed or troop train come through, a dozen reasons, but according to the priorities we were at the bottom of the list. We were locked in the box car. A bunch of American Bombers, bombed us. I didn't know, how many bombs they dropped but a lot hit about fifty or one hundred feet from us and sure gave us, a shake up. Another time, I said: "good bye to all." We had been parked in a rail yard, a guard was sitting at the open door. We jumped over him, out of the box car and ran for about a mile, before they dropped any more. As weak as I was, I sure ran.

Then, we got to the prison camp "Stalag 7a" where I wrote Ginger and you through the Red Cross but I guess they never got far. We got our Red Cross box a week there, they were sure a blessing and a God send. The Germans gave us practically no food at all. Most of the horse meat they did gave us was rotten and couldn't be eaten. By this time Patton was getting close and we began to see the end.

On first part of April, we got notice to pack up. We made pack sack out of underwear top and bottom out of shirts or anything, thousands of us started out on a big march we did not know where. The odd time we slept in a barn at night, but most of the time we slept in a field or in the woods. The Germans give us a loaf and half of bread, a bowl of soup and about four pounds of spuds for 16 days. The rest we bartered, with our cigarettes or soap from the Red Cross parcels, from the German people, mostly farmers. We begged it, swiped it, or any way possible to get it.

But, thank God, for the Red Cross. They had big white trucks with Red Crosses on them and used to bring the Red Cross boxes to us. I had to look after myself, its up to yourself, if you want to eat. Some of us swiped it off the Farmers or the Germans or go hungry. When I had the chance, I didn't go hungry.

We marched in long columns and the Americans would fly over us and think we were German Soldiers and strafe us with 9 mm. machine gun and cannon which sure was terrible. One afternoon, they killed four, wounded four of our bunches. Another group *had 40 killed and a bunch wounded. There was no fun when you know it was your own boys doing it.*

It was harder on our nerves, then flying over Germany with flak and bombs all around. I will take my chance up there in the air dropping them, then down on the ground catching them and getting hit. We were very fortunate, the weather was warm all the time, but on the sixteenth day, we came to the end of our march of 100 miles and arrived at Mooseburg.

We were put behind the barbed wire. The food was pretty good there. We were getting a "Red Cross" box, each week. We were there until that glorious day of April 28, when the Americans 3rd Army had liberated us. It was wonderful the sight of white bread. German bread is almost black and the white bread looked like your "angel food cake." We ate it the same way. Our food got better.

There was a farm just out of camp, with dozens of pigs in it. We killed them all one afternoon; just went with an axe or a knife, chased one until you got it cornered, hit it, bled it. Burn the hair off or cut the rind off, cut it up and carried it home. I had almost a pig head, under my bed. Fried pork for breakfast, dinner and supper. We swiped chickens, eggs, lettuce, carrots, spuds, beets ect. also got American rations and Red Cross boxes. Most of us made ourselves sick by eating to much, but we just couldn't resist, having the foods there and not eating it.

I was the cook for myself and five others we ate good. I swiped the foods and cooked it. All of it, helped pass the time away. The other guys in the were no good for that they were a little bashful. But, the Germans, still own me lots and they wouldn't feed us so, it was up to us to help ourselves.

On Armistice night, we built a huge fire. We put boxes, doors, wooden black out shuttles, tables, benches, chairs, beds, straw, wagons, everything that could be carried and burn; went on to the fire. But it was a little way of celebrating the end.

On May the 08, I walked to "Landshot" (15) and on the tenth flew to Reims. France had lunch there in an American Camp: turkey, green beans, spuds peaches and all I ate, two full dinners in about an hour and a half. It was served to us by German prisoners, which was wonderful, if we wanted more, we hollered at them, to get it. Throw our cigars on the ground, so they would have to pick them up and stepped on it to. We were a little bitter, it will take a while to get over it.

They knew how we had been treated and were sure scared of us. I would love the job of looking after some of them by God. The first night, we landed in England (by air) they had a party for us. All the eggs, bacon, and toast we could eat. Had beer and all. But I never drank much about 6 pints and I was high as a kite and the happiest, I had a big smile on my face. Boy it was great! I spent a couple of days in Bournemouth, got in touch with Ginger and just starting my six weeks leave.

I am not sure what my rank is. But, at least a WO1 or maybe a P.O. Officer. I will know next week. Ginger and I are going

"THE LONG RETURN"

to London and arrange about us going back which will be pretty
soon. Ginger, was wonderful. I think everyone had given up
hopes of every seeing me again, especially, after the news of
January 03. But Ginger kept hoping. She never touched a penny
of our money, every cent was put in the bank. We hope to have
enough to buy a small house and furnish it. When we get back,
so if you hear of anything, look into it because we hope we
will be there in a couple of months.

I guess you got lots of telegrams. I sent 3 and wired flowers. Ginger sent a telegram, and wired flowers, the air ministry should have sent one. But it sure seems funny or queer. I
should say, to read your own mourning letters. The people down
here, are treating me wonderful. Ginger's Mom, getting extra
milk, eggs, all that kind of food, and I am sure eating it.

We are planning to spend a couple of days up at Gladies
place in Manchester, London and all over. We have to start
watching my money, being so long without it and being able to
buy things, well it just burns holes in your pockets. But, I
think I have earned a little bit of a good time.

I eat about 5 times a day, at least or whenever I see food.
I bought Ginger's brother-in-law civilian suit and getting it
tailored to fit, it is a new one, wore only a couple of times
and if I get my " WO1" which I will know this week-end. I am
going to buy a good dress uniform.

My God! has "Nancy" changed! I keep looking at that big
picture of her and she is really cute and I will bet quite a
flirt, she looks a lot like "Betty". I guess, I have also
missed Fred again. I believe he left England a couple of days
ago. I will be seeing him soon. He seems to think quite a lot
of Ginger and I sure hope all the rest of you do to. I am sure
you will.

I have to go to church on Sunday, with Ginger's Mother, but
I guess I have a lot to be thankful for. It was sure a surprise Jean having another baby and it is really swell to have
it named Roberta after me. I guess, Jim may be over soon. I
hope, I don't go back before he gets here. I am sure glad you
and Pop, are still in good health. I guess, you will be moving
out to the ranch pretty soon. Tell Pop, to get lots of roast-
ers, a good young steer, a couple of porkers and lots of vegetables and all.

You will be having Ginger and I there pretty soon. I really
like my eating now. It's great to hear that "Grandma's" still
well and all of you except Granddad with a bad heart, is not
so good. Let "Betty" , "Jean" and all read this, because I may
not have time, to write them a long one. Give my love to Mrs.
" Forest and Pop". You had best send my mail, direct to here,
because I am not sure where I will be. I have still got my
watch but it took a lot of keeping. I have had it on my ankle,
up my sleeves lining of my coat. Not much more because I won't
be able to fit it in the envelope. Mom write real soon a real
long letter, one giving me all the news. I don't know where
"Drum" is? I think the least he could have done was look up

231

Ginger after I went missing. That's all over now, we are having a swell time.
I will write again in London.
Love Bob

Fig.111 A copy of the 17 page hand written letter I wrote my mother when I arrived in London

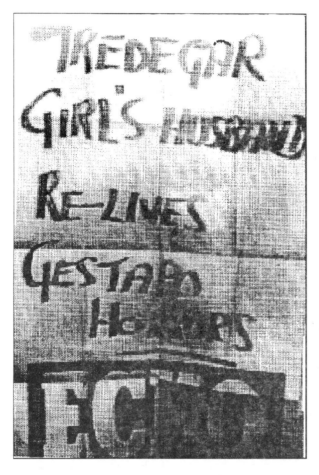

Fig.11m Two by four feet sign on all the streets corners of Tredegar South Wales where my wife lived.

25th of June 1945.
H. Trompstr.
Utrecht. Holland.

Dear Mrs. Porter.

This letter comes from a family, where your husband hid himself, while he was in Holland during the war. We have done our best to find out, if he is still living, for he passed the border at Xmas and we didn't hear anything since. Something terrible has happened to us. My father was arrested on the first day of our liberation as he was accused of working with the Gestapo, which is not true of course. All my father's friends, such as Mr. Rakers, whom your husband knows very well, won't rest before they have my father set free, as it is a great injustice. The Field security believe in my father innocence and therefore he is under their protection. They asked us to try and find your husband and have him write a letter in which he tells how he was treated at our house. Where he stayed, and tell all what he thinks of my father, especially his political views. He has to swear this and have a military stamp on the paper. Will you please see that we will soon get this paper, as they threatened to shoot my Dad, which the Field Security prevented. We would be very thankful, if you would do this for us. We need it very badly and there is great hurry. Our best wishes also to your husband.

Yours truly

Shelah Heitinga

Fig.11n 9 (A copy of a letter from) Shelah Heitinga writing about her Father

23 June 1945.
3 P.R.G.P.
1st Cdn. Army (Overseas.)

Dear Bob,

I am a friend of the Heitinga family with whom you stayed for a time during your hiding in Holland. They have since had, and are now experiencing, a difficult period because Mr. Heitinga has been arrested by the Dutch Underground as a Gestapo agent. This arrest happened the first day we Canadians entered occupied Holland so I have not had the pleasure of speaking to him. However, I met Shelah and Eileen the first day of their liberation and have been almost permanent article in their home ever since.

I personally, as well as our own Canadians Fields Security, who have a helping hand in this Heitinga case, believe Mr. Heitinga is innocent!! It is most urgent (I repeat-most urgent) that we have a signed document with a lawyer's stamp on it, from you, stating what you know of Mr. Heitinga personally.

Tell all you can think of regarding your treatment here in the Heitinga's home. This document will prove Mr. Heitinga's anti-Nazi activities and may serve as a release for him. At the moment we believe that he is being framed so that another individual may go free.

This may be wrong but your statement will help greatly. "Please post the document by Air Mail and Register it as soon as possible"

I guess I should explain that my home is in Regina, Sask., and I am a member of the S.S.R. Let me hear from you post haste because days are precious. That is all I can think of at the moment so until I hear from you I remain,

Yours sincerely

Capt. L.W. Tracy.

P.S. Mrs Heitinga ,

3 P.R.G

Eileen and Shelah send

1 Cdn. Army Overseas

their love and best wishes

Fig.11o (A copy of letter) Capt. Tracy's wanting, a character reference for Mr. Heitinga

Of course Ginger wanted to know what I had been doing and I found out that my sister Jean had had a baby girl whom she named "Roberta", after me. I had missed my brother Fred by a week. He had come to England on his way home from Africa. It was a funny feeling for people to meet me on the street, when they told me they thought I was dead. We went up to the OTU in Stratford-on-Avon where Ginger was stationed and where I had first met her, to visit for a couple of days, then back down to Birmingham and then to Wales.

I received a great welcome home in Wales, with the whole town turning out. There were big signs on the street by the newspaper selling papers. All the neighbours brought their extra rations. Farmers gave us eggs to build me up and get my weight back. I mentioned to someone that I had the urge to have a "gooseberry pie". My God, I had them coming out of my ears! Everybody brought them over. I never mentioned anything else I would like after that.

I received a letter from Shelah Heitinga and one from a Captain Tracy of the Canadian Army. Shelah's father was having great difficulties with the authorities in Holland. I got in touch with the Canadian Army and they got in touch with Captain Tracy. I wanted to go over to Holland and speak for him personally. They didn't think that would help anymore so I wrote everything down on paper, everything I could remember. I had all the information documented by a lawyer to make sure it was all legal, so it could be used in the court in Holland. I felt strongly about this

as the Heitingas had treated me so well. I was posi-
tive he wasn't a traitor. He wouldn't have helped me
twice if he was. He also knew what Rakers was doing
and a lot of Papa's Rakers friends were doing for a
long time. The letters from Shelah and Captain Tracy
are self explanatory.

My six weeks leave soon came to an end and I
had to report back to Bournemouth. Ginger came
down with me and we got a small hotel room . It was
only for a few days and then I got travelling papers to
head back to Canada. I got the ship from Gouroch,
Scotland and I was on my way home. Funny how
things worked. I wanted to stay in England for a while
and there were thousands who wanted to go home,
but I had to go.

Fig.11p Ex-POW out for dinner

Chapter Twelve

Back in Canada

I had my travelling papers ordering me to be in Gouroch, Scotland for July 7th 1945, to return to Canada, but I never got there until the 8th. The ship "Ile de France" was in the harbour ready to leave. They were very displeased with me as I was late and they had all boarded, ready to leave. I figured they would leave me behind which wouldn't have bothered me. But no, they had a little boat and took me out to the ship, and we were on our way back to Canada.

When I came over to England, I travelled on the "Queen Mary" which was fairly new. The "Ile de France" was not. We went over in five days, but it took us almost eight days to get back. The food was a lot better, but maybe I was conditioned to a different food selection than I was two years before when I came over. We landed in Halifax and were put on trains leaving for Vancouver. This was another six days of travelling, but the train service across Canada was great! We travelled first class as most of us were aircrew as well as ex-POW and we were treated just tremendously. I think the cooks were very pleased because we ate everything they gave us.

I had a great welcome coming home. It was great to be home, but it is never as good coming home as one dreams of. When one is away from home, one sort of exaggerates the good things and forgets the bad things. You expect everything to be the same as when you left. I had been away four years and things had changed a lot. Most of the fellows I knew were still overseas or back east and a lot were married with different groups of friends.

I was really surprised to see my little sister Nancy. When I had left home four years ago she was a little ten years old kid. Now she was 14 years old, very cute and grown up. There was a boy next door called W alter and she was kind of sweet on him. If we were outside and he came out of his house I would sing very loud "Walter, Walter, lead me to the altar." It would embarrass her very much. After she raised four children, a couple of divorces and forty years later they got married and are living very happily.

I had been used to a very active life, so I wasn't very good at just sitting around. I was out of the habit of telling my mother where I was going. Ginger was still in England and I didn't know when she would be able to come over. My mother had a bit of a problem understanding. I would say I was going to town and she would say, "When will you be back", I'd say; "I don't know." I enjoyed drinking and I liked to party and didn't know who I was going to run into.

In the first part of August I had a very sad letter from Dicky. Papa had been killed in a car accident with a Canadian Army vehicle. It was almost unbelievable. Here was a man who had been fighting in the Underground for five years, taking so many risks in life and death of situations, then when he

Fig 12a Roger at Rakers' funeral

Fig.12b 21 Gun Salute at Rakers' funeral

Fig.12c The Mayor at Rakers' funeral

was finally free, he was killed in a car accident three months after the end of the war. So I never saw him again. Roger Schjelderup was in occupied Holland at that time, which was a help to Dicky. Papa was given full recognition with a 21 gun salute. Roger was a Captain then and represented the Canadian Army at the funeral. He spoke over the grave. The Lord Mayor, the Underground Commander, the High Officer in the Dutch Police, Slim and many other friends also said their piece. What a shame, after all he had done for Holland, the Dutch people, Canadians like myself, Roger and many others! Not to forget the 195 Jewish people he had helped feed and hide. The risk to his family was so great, and so few people understood what people like Rakers have done.

On Sept. 3rd 1945, after my forty-five day leave was up, I reported to Jericho RCAF Station and started to get my discharge. By September 11th, all the medical and paper work was completed. After four years less fifteen days in the service, I had a medical discharge as I had a few problems. My feet were in bad shape from being on the ice in bare feet the night I was captured on January second.

For bad nerves the treatment you got, you laid down on a bed, and talked about things that had happened to you, trying to get you to the point that bothered you the most and then give you a big shot of electricity. This was called "shock treatment", which wasn't very nice and I don't think it helped. There was a lot of discussions at that time as to whether it was good or not.

They tried many experimental methods and they had lots of guinea pigs to try them on. One fellow was nick-named "Blackie" because he used to black out all the time. He would just go out like a light for a few hours. Another of the guys wouldn't go to sleep without a big baseball bat next to him. We would wait until he went to sleep and then take it from him. My shoulder was still giving me problems from the crash. In the different camps I was in, I had spent a lot of time sleeping on bare cold concrete floors, and so had a lot of aches and pains in my joints.

My nerves hadn't been too bad, but when a couple of orderlies started to give me a shot in the arm when I was getting my discharge a lot of things started to come back to me. I didn't want the needle, but two of them held my arm and gave it to me anyway. I started to shake. That started a reaction and my nerves began to give me big problems. They called it a delayed nervous breakdown.

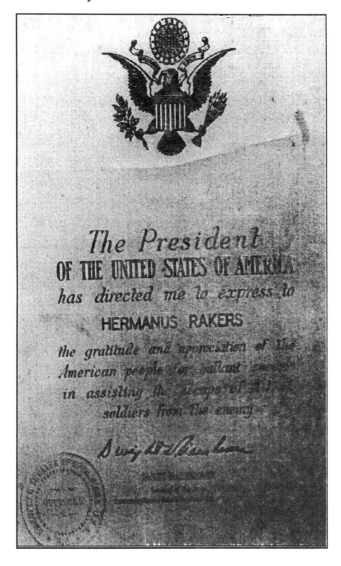

Fig. 12d Rakers' certificate from President Eisenhower

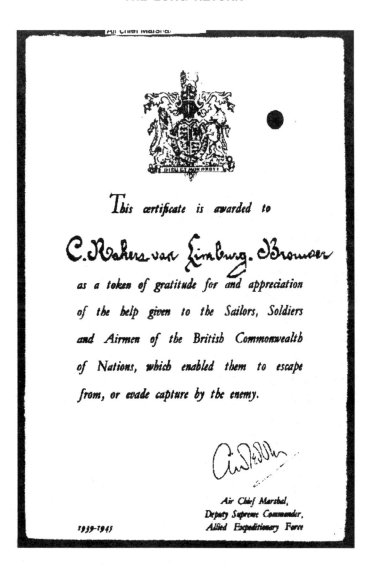

This certificate is awarded to

C. Rahus van Limburg. Brouwer

as a token of gratitude for and appreciation of the help given to the Sailors, Soldiers and Airmen of the British Commonwealth of Nations, which enabled them to escape from, or evade capture by the enemy.

Air Chief Marshal,
Deputy Supreme Commander,
Allied Expeditionary Force

1939-1945

Fig. 12e Dicky's Certificate from the Air chief Marshal

At times, I would start to shake, couldn't hold a glass to my lips, and even had problems eating. Then another little problem came up. Before I was shot down, I owed the Sergeant's mess "Four shillings and six pence". That is about one dollar and six cents. This bill had stayed in my file all this time. I didn't think I should pay for this, as surely, when one is shot down and away for a whole year, they could cancel this tiny amount. Maybe it was the way they approached me with it, but I told them they could go to hell. They said, "If you don't pay it, it will hold up your discharge." That was the least of my worries, I told them that I still wouldn't pay it, and I got my discharge anyway.

I spent the next few months in Shaughnessy Hospital (The Canadian military hospital) trying to get my nerves settled down. There was a bunch of us in the same shape with a lot of different psychiatrists. I was assigned to Dr Hutton who I thought was great! The medical authorities had different methods that they used. One was that they would have you lying One fellow took off in his pyjamas and, with only a blanket around him, headed to town. We chased after him, down Oak Street, and caught him just as he was getting on a bus. The ward we were in was called the "nutty ward" and I guess they had good reason to call it that. We were all a little nutty at that time. I always figured I wasn't that bad, it was just the other fellows, but sometimes I wonder.

Ginger came to Canada and we were settling down when I had another bad period. I went back into the hospital again for another month, and slowly everything got better.

In the early 1950s, when I was in Toronto, I met Shelah and Mr. Heitinga. They had immigrated to

Canada. Mr. Heitinga wasn't feeling very well. He never got over his time in prison and how the Dutch people had treated him after the war. A couple of years later his wife died and I lost track of Shelah. That was too bad as I like to keep in touch with people.

In 1952, I got a letter from Frits, the fellow who had picked me up on the side of the road the night I was shot down. He sent it to the family of RE. Porter as he thought I had been killed the night of Jan. 2nd. It was amazing how I ever got this letter. My family had moved from this address seven years before. The postman mentioned this strange letter to my grandmother, across the street. My grandmother said, "That's my grandson", so I was very lucky to get it. I don't think I would have a chance in hell of ever getting it delivered today. Things have changed. Frits sent some things I had left with him when I first got to Holland, including the silk escape map of Holland, as well as other articles which were part of my escape kit, plus a few personal things. In 1955 Frits came over to Canada on Dutch immigration business, so we had a couple of days to reminisce. I was building a house at the time and working in the basement. He called out in Dutch, "I am English, can you hide me." It made me have goose pimples all over me again.

It was a great day to remember. What a good talk we had. I found out what had happened to all the different people I had met but never heard from.

In 1958 Ginger, my son Les, my daughter Shelley and I went to Holland for a visit. Unbelievable memories! We met Klaas and Ans Middelkoop, who kept me for a couple of weeks in their house in 1944. The apartment above the bank was still their home. Les was thirteen years old and Shelley was nine, their oldest son Kees, was a little older than Les, and their other two daughters Edith and Jacqueline were about the same age. While we were talking inside the house, the children were playing outside. Klaas and Ans' children couldn't speak English and ours couldn't speak Dutch, but they played together all afternoon.

Dicky is living in Zutphen now, and her two sons, Hans and Theo had grown up. They were both away working, so I didn't see them at all, but we met a lot of other people I had known.

We went with Dicky to see the house I had lived in, in Groningen, and my hiding place was still there. The people living in the house didn't even know about it and hadn't known anything about the history of the house during the war. We visited the cemetery where my crew were buried, and spent a while there just thinking back to a different time and how easily it could have been me buried there.

After spending seven months with (Mamma) Dicky, in Holland in 1944, and writing back and forth for twenty-five years, she came over to Canada for a visit. We re-lived many days, had a great holiday and it gave me a chance to pay back a little to one great lady! Over the years Dicky and I have kept in contact. Dicky came over to Canada four times and I went back to Holland five or six times. Each time I was over I would meet someone else I had met in 1944.

"THE LONG RETURN"

R.G. van der Haar   3.VI. '52
Steven van der Hagenlaan 2,
Amersfoort - Holland.

Family R.E. Porter
3406 Imperial Street
New Westminster, Vancouver B.C. CANADA

Dear Mr. and Mrs. Porter,

Enclosed I send you some objects of your son Sergeant Porter, whom I met in Holland during the last war. I found these things in a garret cabinet, in which I after the war put away several souvenirs from the last time of war and which I have no more seen into since that time. When my wife cleared away this case recently, she met among other things these objects.

I do not know if you have ever heard something about your son and for that reason I shall write you what I know about him.

One rainy morning I think it was about May-June '44 - I rode on my bicycle from Zeist to Driebergen (two villages in the province of Utrecht) when suddenly there came a person out of the bushes at the edge of the wood, who beckoned me to stop. When I complied with this request, he showed me a little yellow book, in which were found some Dutch sentences, among others things the question: Can you hide me ? (In Dutch: Kunt U mej verbergen?)

I shall never forget the manner, in which your son pronounced this little Dutch sentence. At once I understood that he was a flyer, who had been dropped in the last night, the more as in this night there had been an air fight above these villages. Because there was a great deal of treason during the years of occupation, I asked him in broken English: Show me other things, so that I am convinced you are indeed an Englishman. Then it was evident that he was a Canadian. I put him on the back of my bicycle and we rode to Driebergen (Three-mountains) where I had some friends, who took further care of him. I believe that one of them, Mr. K. van Middelkoop, wrote to you.

Some days later I had been arrested by the Germans and I was put in prison for an other affair. After three months I was set free and after that I still met your son occasionally at Groenekan (municipality Maartensdijk) at the house of Mr. and Mrs. Rakers. Because I was removed I lost sight of him. A long time after the war, I heard that your son presumably was taken prisoner by the Germans and had perished. I think, that Mr. Middelkoop gave you further information about this event.

During the war I met very many airmen and other pilots in hiding, so that I cannot remember your son very well. The only thing I remember was that he told me at our first meeting, that he first wanted to stop some girls. He presumed that they were schoolgirls, because they all wore a black cap with an orange band. Because he was by military orders only allowed to accost a single person, he refrained from doing so. That was very fortunate, for these children were of the " jeugdstorm", a youth organization in our country, which was on friendly terms with the Germans. These girls would have certainly given up your son to the Germans or have warned the police.

I suppose that you will appreciate the possession of these simple objects. It is a last souvenir of your son and of the country, where your son offered his life for the sake of liberty. We owe great thanks to your nation and in it to your son for the important contribution to the rescue and liberation from the German army and occupation, and we pay respectful homage to those, who offered their lives for this sake. I hope that you will be so kind as to write me if these things .

With kind regards,
Yours respectfully,

R.G. van der Haar

Fig.12f Letter from Frits the man who first picked me up. He sent it six years after the war ended

247

Fifty Years Later

Fig.12g Roger before he died in September 29th 1972

Fig.12h I married France Clémence St-Amand on July 5th 1992. This picture was taken on our wedding day. I call her "Fran"

Chapter Thirteen

Fifty Years Later

Our big trip back to Holland was in May 1995 for the 50 year anniversary of the end of the war. W e spent a very memorable month there.

Fig.13a Alf Thompson and I in the big 1995 parade at Apeldoorn in Holland

We will never again see a country showing their appreciation to another country as the Dutch people showed to we Canadians. One parade at Apeldoorn lasted over three hours. Attended by 200,000 Dutch people of all ages, young and old. There were more than sixteen thousand organised Canadian veterans, plus a hundred like myself that went over on our own, to celebrate with the Dutch people. Those that went over in organised groups were put up by the Dutch people, in their homes, in the cities and towns. Their hosts kept them, fed them, and got them to all the celebrations. Things were very well organised. Parking lots were organised in the fields, on each highway, a few miles before the town where the parade was going to be.

Fig.13b Parade at Groesbeek Cemetery

They had hundreds of buses taking us into the town. You would take note of the number of the bus you got on and when it was over you looked for the bus with the right number and it would take you back to the parking place where you were picked up.

I don't know what would have happened if you forgot the number of yours! The Dutch have a organisation called "Keep Them Rolling." These volunteers each have a Canadian World War II truck, motorcycle, tank or some sort of war vehicle that they have restored. The vehicles had been either abandoned or sold by the army. They had 5,000 of these and used many of them in the parade to carry a lot of the older veterans; those who couldn't walk the two or three miles.

Fig.13c My Crews Grave taken May 4 1995. Wybe Buising and I

Many started to walk and were picked up along the way. The weather was very warm at that time, which didn't help, and many of these army veterans were eighty years of age or over. We had a very large memorial service at Groesbeek Cemetery where thousands of Canadians are buried. There must have been more than a hundred buses of veterans. Volunteers served us free refreshments and food.

On May 4th, we were again at Amersfoort Cemetery where my crew are buried. It is a large cemetery where hundreds of soldiers and airmen are buried from several different countries. My crew is buried in a row and the graves are kept in beautiful condition . The cemetery is kept just like a park, mostly done by school children. On this day, every year, the school children put flowers on all the graves. It was very touching and moving.

Wybe Buising, a Dutch fellow who helped me with a lot of my research, had contacted the Warden of "Wolvenplein Prison" in Utrecht and talked him into giving me a tour. I had spent a number of weeks there with the Gestapo after I was captured. It is now run as an ordinary prison.

The Warden wasn't there the day I went, but his secretary gave me a full tour. I visited the cell where I had spent so much time and saw the black hole where I had been put in solitary, as well as the so-called exercise yard. I couldn't take pictures inside but took these of the yard and of what I saw out the window and from the outside. It wasn't a nice place, but it had been fixed up a lot since I was in there.

I spent a lot of time with Dicky and her family. You more than likely know, by this time, that I have a tremendous respect for her and owe her so very much. At eighty-six years old, she was still tall and very proud. If you offered to help her, she would just look down at you. She lives alone in her apartment, but her son Theo and her daughter-in- law Beth live close by and are very good to Dicky. Her grandchildren Yvonne and Ronnie are also there for her. Dicky and I had some great drives around the country, to places we had been in and seen fifty years before. We did a lot of reminiscing.

Fig.13d Dicky, May 1997

Fig.13e Vonny, her Husband Hank and I, Fifty Years later

We re-lived so many things, we have something between us that very few people will ever have. W e visited my friend Vonny, just as good looking as she was fifty years ago! Her husband Hank had died a couple of years before. We had a good time talking about things that had happened fifty years ago. W e talked about the time when Hank was in hiding (he didn't want to go to forced labour in Germany.) A friend of theirs was getting married, so Hank dressed up as a girl and went to the wedding. On their way home a couple of German solders tried to pick them both up!

I also had some lunches to reminisce with Klaas and Ans van Middelkoop. They drove me around to many places re-living my life there: we stopped at the river where I crossed in the little boat, and had to help the German soldiers push the boat off the bank; we went around to the brickyard where I had been captured and took pictures of it; we found the town where I was first interrogated. We drove around and saw many memorials to the war. Klaas showed me the house where he went into hiding when the Germans came after him. He only had time to take a few personal things and just had to disappear. He took a new name, lived in a new town, had a new identity but no job. They had to finish the last six months of the war this way. I met some great people in my seven months in Holland and these are two at the top of my list.

Fig.13f Klaas, Ans, Kees and I. Fifty Years later. Kees was a baby when I was there

They are now retired and Klaas spends his time with ex-underground people that need help. I had lunch with Eep Bos (The Teacher) and his lady friend. He was the one that first interrogated me fifty years ago.

Fig.13g Theo and his wife Beth, Dicky and my wife Fran-Clemence

Fig.13h Eep Bos fifty years later.

I wore his clothes and he wore my uniform, that he had dyed. It was a great re-union! Unfortunately, he was sick for a couple of weeks and sadly missed most of the celebrations. I met Nellie and her father Mr. Cornelissen. He is ninety-six and in great shape! He lives in a little house at the back of Nellie and her husband's home. I just hope I am in as good shape at that age. What great people came out of the Underground!

I lost track of the Heitingas until this year. On a CD and the internet with all the telephone numbers in Canada and the USA, I found that their step-mother was living in Sooke, BC. John Heitinga had moved to Canada in 1950. He spent most of his life in Ontario as an artist and doing scenery art for the stages of the National Ballet and the Grand Stand Show for the Canadian National Exhibition.

Fig.13i Nellie Cornelissen, myself and her father ninety-six years old.

Fig.13j Shelah Heitinga and myself fifty years later

Fig.13k Eileen Heitinga and myself fifty years later

Fig. 131 Doc van Veelen and myself fifty years later. He is 90 years old and does his own gardening.

I found Shelah and Eileen Heitinga, living in California and I got their phone numbers. Eileen is living in Hollywood. I visited them both this year, we had a great day talking. Shelah is living in Newport Beach. I visited them both and had a good day of reminiscing. Shelah had the newspaper press with photographers and all. We had our picture on the full front page in color in the Newport Beach newspaper. The headlines read "Former WW2 airman meets daughter of Dutch Resistance member after fifty years." That made me feel like a celebrity. Doctor van Veelen, our doctor in the Underground is ninety years old. He has at least an acre of beautiful garden that he looks after by himself. His wife, about the same age, with help looks after the house. These are terrific people. He arranged the nurse for Roger Schjelderup and looked after him when he was really sick. He also came around to visit me a couple of times.

I lost track of Jan Bakker but I believe he is now retired and living in Diemen in the Netherlands.

Fig.13m *Louis Trainor Died in Prince Edward Island. February 1997*

Fig. 13n *Wilf Berry 50 years later, looking good. Retired and living in Mission BC*

The CBC television show

"The Valour and the Horror"

They talked about what the air force did in the war. This show was a very big insult to all of us who flew in WW II. My parting word is an article (Excerpted from Bill Gunston's Introduction to "So Many"). It says a lot more than I could ever write. This was reproduced in "Flarepath" a news- letter of The Bomber Harris Trust. This article is repro- duced with the permission of Bill Gunston.

Without the bombers, what?

(Excerpted from Bill Gunston's Introduction to so Many)

On December 18, 1939, a formation of 24 Wellingtons was intercepted by fighters off the German coast; ten were quickly shot down, and only three returned unscathed. This at last convinced the Air Staff that not even a well-disciplined formation of modern bombers could survive in daylight. But switching to night operations was a daunting prospect, be- cause it had not been planned for. The Butt Report, of August 1941, concluded that, on average, one-third of all crews failed to get anywhere near the target.

On February 23, 1942, Air Marshall Sir Arthur Harris was appointed C-in-C of Bomber Command. Morale began to improve at once. When he took over, the twin-engine "heavies" were already being replaced by the bigger Stirling, Halifax and Lancaster. Equally important, the Telecommunications Research

"THE LONG RETURN"

Establishment was at last developing electronic aids which would enable crews to find their targets.

First came Gee, which covered north-west Europe with an invisible lattice of intersecting signals sent from three stations in south-east England...then, in December 1942, the most precise aid of all, Oboe. Again relying on signals from Britain, out to a radius of some 400 km (250 miles), this could guide aircraft with an accuracy of some 100 meters.

In January 1943 bombers began using H_2S. It was heavy, disrupted bomber production, made it impossible to fit the turret or even a window to defend against a night fighter underneath, and behaved like a lighthouse broadcasting the bomber's position to those same night fighters. It was also extremely difficult to use, but it had the advantage that it could not be jammed by the enemy, went wherever the bomber went and, in the hands of a skilled operator, enabled bombs or target indicators to be dropped accurately even over unbroken mist or cloud.

The Pathfinder Force (PFF) began operating from August 1942. Their marking, by Lancasters using H2S and Mosquitoes with Obeo, absolutely transformed Bomber Command's operations. As the striking power of the force grew, so did Harris' leadership not only keep morale sky-high but he insisted on trying to get more aircraft over the target in the shortest time, and thus saturate the defences and allow more aircraft to return unscathed.

Bomber Command's attacks, initially a mere nuisance, became what Hitler's armaments minister, Albert Speer, called "the greatest battle that we lost.". On May 15, 1940, 93 bombers set out for the Krupp works at Essen. In a later assessment it was calculated that the proportion of bombs that actually hit the vast factories was 3 percent. In contrast, in a massive attack by 705 "heavies" on July 25, 1943, marked by Oboe-equipped Pathfinders, the proportion was assessed at 96 percent.

The camaraderie of the crew was crucial. Morale was sustained by the knowledge that one was part of the best crew in Bomber Command which almost everyone believed he was. Who were these aircrew? In many squadrons anyone as old as 25 might be called grandpa, and have to serve as a father-confessor, or as CO pass on sad news to next of kin. Family background counted for nothing. Ability, and the ability to inspire confidence in others, counted for everything... Rare indeed was the crew who doubted the worth of one of their number. And not least of the remarkable factors is that the surviving crews, who became closely knit into a single instantly reacting unit, were made up of a mix of nationalities, ranks and family backgrounds.

In the 1930s nobody could have foreseen that soon Britain would be isolated off the shore of a German-held continent, nor that it would be possible for Bomber Command to lose more than 500 aircrew in a single night. The beleaguered wartime island could never have trained aircrew in anything remotely like the numbers needed, yet it is surely remarkable that this gigantic (Commonwealth Air Training) plan should by late 1944 have trained 131,553 aircrew in Canada, 23,262 in Australia, 16,857 in South Africa, 8235 in Rhodesia, 2,891 in New Zealand and over 13,000 (all pilots) in the USA. Most of this enormous output then came to Britain to be honed to operational standard.

It may be difficult for people whose experience of flying has been in modern airliners or light aircraft to imagine the harshness of a wartime bomber. A Whitney pilot recalls " Rain used to come into the cockpit, and for three months my hands were frost-bitten. " Everywhere was bare metal, with numerous sharp corners, and vital switches that were all too easy to brush against, especially when one's bulk was inflated by the multiple layers of clothing needed to keep out the freezing cold, plus a yellow " Mae West" around the upper body for flotation. A leather helmet covered the head, bulging with the vital earphones. Goggles were issued, but seldom needed. Except for the eyes, the face was covered by a carefully fitted mask which contained a microphone and supplied life-giving oxygen. For air-gunners, one of the layers of clothing would be electrically heated, plugged into the aircraft supply.

When it was all over, of the men who flew with Bomber Command at the start of the war, over 90 percent had been killed. Even those who became operational after D-Day, June 6, 1944, suffered almost 50 percent casualties. Many people, and certainly RAF fighter pilots, felt that Bomber Command should received a special campaign medal. It was possible for a man to complete a whole Tour normally calculated at 30 operations to defended targets and receive no decoration whatsoever apart from the medals automatically given to all aircrew who completed a single operation, such as the Aircrew Europe Star.

What is incontestable is that, over the past 50 years, the role of Bomber Command has been repeatedly analysed and questioned on moral grounds. One veteran recently said" At the end of the War, I was a hero; today I am a mass-murderer."...

It is difficult to write with dispassionate objectivity. Even if one sticks strictly to facts, today's media have shown how easily "facts" can be manipulated and distorted. Despite this, it is at least possible to give a flavour of how people thought 50 years ago.

By 1941 cities throughout Europe had been bombed by the Luftwaffe, and helpless refugees had been machine-gunned from the air. These missions were flown with the sole objective of terrorising the civilian population, and breaking any will to resist. In 1940-42 the Luftwaffe devastated London, Coventry, Southampton, Bristol, Plymouth, Sheffield, Liverpool, Car-

"THE LONG RETURN"

diff, Glasgow and many other British cities. From April 1942
its raids on Britain were specifically redirected against
cities distinguished by three stars in the Baedeker guidebook
as being "of outstanding historic or artistic interest."

By 1941 the United Kingdom was isolated as the only part
of Europe still holding out against Hitler. Ringed by U-boats
and suffering heavy air attack, it had no means of hitting
back except by Bomber Command.

Bomber Command's targets were selected by the War Cabinet,
who were themselves influenced by the suggestions of the Ministry of Economic Warfare. The Commander-in-Chief, who from
February 22, 1942 was Sir Arthur Harris, could not dictate
policy (though he could offer advice). His duty was to assign
targets and units to carry out the orders given to him.

Nobody can reduce to tidy arithmetic the overall effect of
the devastation of Germany, nor what might have been done had
the same effort been applied to some other method of waging
war (but what?). Common sense surely tells us that, without
the sustained attacks on Hitler's war machine, D-Day could
not have taken place in 1944, or that if it had, it might
have been a costly failure. In any case, without Bomber Command, and the equally courageous daytime attacks by the US 8th
Army Air Force, it is difficult to imagine what could have
been a viable alternative.

Today few people have any idea of the tremendous role
played by Bomber Command in winning the war. How many know
that, because it destroyed the majority of the huge barges
Hitler expected would bring his armies to invade Britain losing 718 aircrew in the process, compared with 497 by Fighter
Command even if the Battle of Britain has been lost, a successful invasion would almost certainly have been impossible?
Without any public adulation, Bomber Command then sank seven
of Hitler's 15 major warships, annihilated his merchant fleet
and destroyed or "contracepted" hundreds of his U-boats.

Hitler's production czar, Albert Speer, said "The bombing
of Germany deprived the German forces of 75 percent of their
heavy anti-tank-guns, scattered all over Germany because we
never knew where the bombers would strike next. Field Marshal
Milch had 900,000 fit soldiers manning those guns. In addition, hundreds of thousands of expert tradesmen could not be
called up into the Army because their skills were needed to
repair bomb damage." Dr. Horst Borg, Chief Historian in the
Military History Office in Freiburg, notes that "the alumin-
ium in the fuses of the flak shells would have built 40,000
additional fighter aircraft."

Nobody can say how many British lives were saved by the
attack on the rocket laboratory at Peenemünde, and on the
flying-bomb transport network and launch sites, but it must
be many thousands. When the Allied armies were well estab-
lished in France after D-Day Field Marshal Rommel said "Stop
the bombers or we can't win!" Nobody can say how many British

soldiers were saved by bombing Le Havre; the city was taken, giving the Allies their first Channel port at the cost of 30 British troops, whilst rounding up 11,000 demoralised Germans. Bombers stopped Sepp Dietrich's armour in the Ardennes (the Battle of the Bulge) by cutting all his supply routes; Gen. Dietrich later said " Not even the best troops in the world can stand up to this heavy bombing."

Repeatedly, whenever the Allied armies were held up by stubborn resistance, Bomber Command was always on call to eliminate the opposition. Their culminating achievement in such operations was to allow the British Army to cross the Rhine at Wesel with just 36 casualties, instead of the thousands which had been expected.

Yet, once it was clear that victory was in sight, the decision was taken apparently at the highest level in the British Government to distance itself from the strategic bombing campaign carried out by Harris under its own Ministers' orders. It seems that, with hindsight, the politicians saw that Bomber Command's destruction of Germany might later prove to be an embarrassment, and that therefore it would be convenient for its collective bravery, dedication and sacrifice to be unrecognised and unrewarded.

Today's media naturally reflect the change in public opinion, but that does not excuse a rewriting of history. This has caused distress to those who actually made it, and in 1992 the problem became particularly acute in Canada. Canada's contribution to Bomber Command had been enormous, in training aircrew, in providing aircrew, and in building Hampdens, Lancasters and Mosquitoes. Canadians have the right to feel proud of the giant role their country played in winning the War, but now, as one veteran put it, "We are made to appear as moronic mass-murderers and nut cases."

Canadian veterans were so incensed by what they saw as a gross and deliberate misrepresentation of their war role that they resorted to legal action in an attempt to restore at least a vestige of truth. Hurtful though all this has been to those who suffered and survived, they find it a comfort to see that those who choose to hold opinions contrary to true history are nevertheless free to broadcast those opinions.

They are able to do this because 55,573 men of Bomber Command gave their lives in order that future generations should not be slaves under the Swastika but should enjoy such freedom. We owe it to them to preserve a record of what they really did, what they really thought and felt, and what kind of people they really were.

"THE LONG RETURN"

To order a book please send in "ORDER FORM" to
Bob Porter #2603- 4288 Grange St. Burnaby BC V5H 1P2 CAN.
Write---Phone---Fax--- or---E-mail

Name _____

Address _____

City _____

_____ Prov. or State _____

Country _____ Postal Code _____

Qt.	Title	US. Price	Can. Price	Total
	THE LONG RETURN	**14.95**	**19.95**	
	Shipping and handling (add $4.00 for the first book,			
	$3.00 each additional book) European Shipping		**$4.50 US**	
	Sales tax (G.S.T) (7%. Canadian residence only)		$1.40	
			Total Enclosed	

Telephone Orders	**Fax Orders**
Call 604-433-3237	604-433-2722
Have your Visa or Master card ready	Fill out order blank and fax

E-mail orders boport@intergate.bc.ca
(Give your Visa or Master card number)

Payment : Please Check One
Check   ☐   Credit Card ☐ Money Order   ☐

Visa   ☐   Master Card ☐

Card # _____ Exp. Date _____

Signature _____

Name on Card _____

Quantity discounts are available
For more information call Bob Porter at 604-433-3237
Thank you for your order!
I understand that I can return this book for a full refund if not satisfied
To order a book please send in "ORDER FORM" to

**To order a book please send in "ORDER FORM" to
Bob Porter #2603- 4288 Grange St. Burnaby BC V5H 1P2 CAN.
Write---Phone---Fax--- or---E-mail**

Name

Address

City

_____ Prov. or State _____

Country _____ Postal Code _____

Qt.	Title	US. Price	Can. Price	Total
	THE LONG RETURN	14.95	19.95	

Shipping and handling (add $4.00 for the first book,

$3.00 each additional book) European Shipping **$4.50 US**

Sales tax (G.S.T) (7%. Canadian residence only) $1.40

Total Enclosed

Telephone Orders
Call 604-433-3237
Have your Visa or Master card ready

Fax Orders
604-433-2722
Fill out order blank and fax

E-mail orders boport@intergate.bc.ca
(Give your Visa or Master card number)

Payment : Please Check One

Check ☐ Credit Card ☐ Money Order ☐

Visa ☐ Master Card ☐

Card # _____ Exp. Date _____

Signature _____

Name on Card _____

Quantity discounts are available
For more information call Bob Porter at 604-433-3237
Thank you for your order!
I understand that I can return this book for a full refund if not satisfied

ORDER FORM

To order a book please send in "ORDER FORM" to
Bob Porter #2603- 4288 Grange St. Burnaby BC V5H 1P2 CAN.
Write---Phone---Fax--- or---E-mail

Name _____

Address _____

City

_____ Prov. or State _____

Country _____ Postal Code _____

Qty	Title	US. Price	Can. Price	Total
	THE LONG RETURN	14.95	19.95	
Shipping and handling (add $4.00 for the first book, $3.00 each additional book) European Shipping **$4.50** US				
Sales tax (G.S.T) (7%. Canadian residence only) $1.40				
			Total Enclosed	

Telephone Orders
Call 604-433-3237
Have your Visa or Master card ready

Fax Orders
604-433-2722
Fill out order blank and fax

E-mail orders
boport@intergate.bc.ca Give your Visa or Master card number

Payment : Please Check One

Check ☐   Credit Card ☐   Money Order ☐

Visa ☐   Master Card ☐

Card # _____ Exp. Date _____

Signature _____
Name on Card _____

Quantity discounts are available
For more information call Bob Porter at 604-433-3237
Thank you for your order!
I understand that I can return this book for a full refund if not satisfied

ORDER FORM

To order a book please send in "ORDER FORM" to
Bob Porter #2603- 4288 Grange St. Burnaby BC V5H 1P2 CAN.
Write---Phone---Fax--- or---E-mail

Name

Address

City

_____ Prov. or State _____

Country _____ Postal Code _____

Qty	Title	US. Price	Can. Price	Total
	THE LONG RETURN	14.95	19.95	

Shipping and handling (add $4.00 for the first book,
$3.00 each additional book) European Shipping **$4.50 US**

Sales tax (G.S.T) (7%. Canadian residence only) $1.40

Total Enclosed

Telephone Orders	**Fax Orders**
Call 604-433-3237	604-433-2722
Have your Visa or Master card ready	Fill out order blank and fax

E-mail orders
boport@intergate.bc.ca Give your Visa or Master card number

Payment : Please Check One

Check ☐   Credit Card ☐   Money Order ☐

Visa ☐   Master Card ☐

Card # _____ Exp. Date _____

Signature _____
Name on Card _____

Quantity discounts are available
For more information call Bob Porter at 604-433-3237
Thank you for your order!
I understand that I can return this book for a full refund if not satisfied